SEX
FERTILITY AND
BIRTH CONTROL

SEX
FERTILITY AND
BIRTH
CONTROL

Isadore Rossman, Ph. D., M.D.

Medical Director, Department of
Home Care and Extended Services
Montefiore Hospital and Medical
Center, New York, New York

Stravon Educational Press · **New York**

Book Design by Morton Garchik
Manufactured in the United States of America

Contents

This book is affectionately dedicated to
Dr. George W. Bartelmez, Emeritus Professor of Anatomy
at the University of Chicago School of Medicine

He taught us all the exultation of understanding
Nature, and the disciplined labor needed
by those who would know her secrets

List of Figures, Charts, and Tables

Sex, Fertility, and Birth Control

Introduction

As its title indicates, this book deals with sex and reproduction and surveys the natural facts, as well as the man-made factors which control them. Among the topics considered are the variable functioning of the sex organs, the limiting factors on reproduction as imposed by woman's fertility, the contributions of the male's sexual performance, the pregnancy potential of married couples, and the various birth control methods, some good, some bad, which are currently in use to change this potential. Although reproduction is a common enough event, accurate knowledge of many of its aspects is quite uncommon. Because human sexuality long suffered from the most severe taboos, many important and fundamental facts have only recently been discovered. Indeed some of the material discussed in these pages has been learned only in the past few years. Here and there the material necessarily verges on the technical, but I have tried to keep all such descriptions as simple and understandable as possible.

Sex, Fertility, and Birth Control

For a number of reasons sex has long been a forbidden area. Some have felt that sexuality was too private and intimate a subject to be discussed in detail in a publicly distributed book, and have thus contributed to the conspiracy of silence. For the effect of exercising such a ban was to substitute word-of-mouth inaccuracy, haphazardly transmitted, for accurate written statements disseminated in a more open manner. Furthermore, the attempt to keep the facts secret ran head on into the overriding reality of the need for such information. The ostrich may bury his head ever deeper in the sands but the real world does not disappear as a result. Women who find themselves almost continuously pregnant, or pregnant after alleged precautions, are not likely after a time to believe that ignorance is bliss.

Others have hesitated to endorse a wide dissemination of this knowledge, somehow feeling that calling attention to the biological or technical aspects of sexuality would in some manner detract from the warmth and beauty of it. To them it should be said that the biological does not detract from the psychic. Love continues to be a supreme, even overpowering emotion, whether one is knowledgeable or ignorant of sexuality. And, in fact, the experience of marriage counselors indicates that sexual ignorance may be the major barrier to a happy marriage.

Although much is said about the sexual revolution of our time, the doctor is likely to feel that the Victorian and Puritan traditions are still very much alive. Much is still left undone and unsaid. If at least a modicum of sexual knowledge is important and basic, one would suppose that it should be taught to young adults at some point. Although one may show considerable hesitation over content and phraseology at the grammar school level, it is hard to account for similar omission at the high school, and even more difficult, at the college levels. The failure of our educational system, even with the maturing and the mature who are already faced by a variety of gnawing problems, is well known. Even courses in biology tend to skirt the issue, leading to the familiar jokes about "the birds, bees, and the flowers." The gap between the birds and the bees and human beings corresponds to millions of years in the natural kingdom and the gap continues to be reflected in the educational kingdom. It is often said that the necessary additional information above the "birds and bees" level can be secured from parents, and that in fact this is one of the necessary roles of parenthood. Many parents, however, find teaching the facts of life embarrassing or difficult and most frequently treat the subject by omission. When both parents and the educational system falter, little is left except the printed word, and the contribution that books can make becomes clearer and even more important.

Bad though the situation has been concerning information on human sexuality, the status of birth control information has been even worse. In fact, until very recently, some of our states had laws forbidding the free dissemination of such knowledge. This was the case in such otherwise culturally advanced states as Connecticut and Massachusetts, where the letter of the law forbade doctors to instruct their patients in birth control methods. This was the situation that persisted until June 7, 1965, when the United States Supreme Court decreed that a state legislature could not pass legislation which invaded the privacy of the marriage bedroom. It seems rather startling to find, almost two centuries after the American and French Revolutions had proclaimed the rights of the individual, that the state should claim a right to interfere with strictly private marital decisions. But the saddest aspect of all this recent legal history was the gap between custom and law and the onrushing population crisis. In a world already all but overwhelmed by that crisis there is tragedy rather than stupidity in the arrest of a Yale Medical School professor for fitting a woman with a contraceptive device.

Sex, Fertility, and Birth Control

The author is convinced that knowledge of the basic facts of human reproduction and of its control should be part of everyone's fundamental information. If only on the basis of the long-cherished concept that the proper study of man is man, the area of reproduction can hardly be left untouched. Onrushing national and world events alone will make it necessary for every well-educated person to know what an intrauterine coil is or what the many pros and cons of birth control pills are. Further, it appears that such knowledge will soon be regarded as a necessity and generally taught rather than be left as an option for the inquisitive and the intelligent to learn. Since family planning is now at long last considered a proper area of governmental concern at the national and even the municipal level, some of the last important barriers to free dissemination of information and knowledge are crumbling. This volume is written in the hope of further contributing to the spread of this basic and important knowledge.

It need hardly be said that a discussion of some technical or factual aspects of sex does not reduce human sexuality to the level of technology. The scientific aspects of human reproduction have nothing to do with the emotional or poetic facts of human love. Absence of reference to the lyric and romantic in this book indicates neither conscious neglect nor intentional disrespect. Sexuality is a force which can encompass both scientific prose and the sweep of poetry. When all is said and done, sex and reproduction are the basis of the family, which in turn is the mainstay of society. Both family and society will flourish better in an atmosphere of enlightenment than in one of ignorance.

ISADORE ROSSMAN, M.D.

The Basis
of Fertility:
SEXUALITY

1.
The Facts of Life: Some Basic Questions and Answers

From many points of view—biological, psychological, or just plain interpersonal—the most notable achievement of one's lifetime is that of reproduction. Having a child is—or should be—an act of love and an expression of the most profound of instincts. But more than that, it initiates the most durable and rewarding of all relationships, that of parent to child. Furthermore, it is the only manifest road to immortality. No matter what else happens, that part of an individual represented in the offspring goes on. And however modified and diluted, at least a little part of that individual will be there, and functioning centuries from now, in someone in whom some physical and perhaps mental characteristics will be the very ones handed on. Though reproduction has occurred innumerable times over tens of thousands of years, and though wise men have studied it for centuries, it remains the strangest and most complex event in our world.

Sex, Fertility, and Birth Control

The forming of a new human being has an impetus and complexity that baffles analysis. Human birth is the culmination of nine months of the most feverish and mysterious building process in the universe. It all starts with the fusion of two tiny cells, a meeting that unleashes prodigious forces perhaps to be compared to the explosive outbursts when atoms collide. In every sense a little miracle occurs when the sperm and egg cells meet.

It is still a fact that the further backward one goes from the time of the birth, the greater the tendency to conceal relevant facts and thus the greater the ignorance of those who contribute to it. In contrast to the publicity, the announcements, the rejoicing that occur at the time of the birth, the pregnancy that precedes it may be regarded somewhat furtively, even concealed. And the existence of the sexuality that generated all this is traditionally cloaked in darkness and complete mystery. The sexual act of course should be a private and intimate event. But privacy does not mean shamefacedness, nor does secrecy require ignorance. Unfortunately, certain social attitudes, together with educational neglect, have resulted in many couples going into marriage so lacking in elementary sex knowledge that ignorance interferes with bliss. Since sexual activity and pregnancy are inevitable concomitants of marriage, one would suppose that at least the basic facts would be known to participants in the wedding ceremony. But despite some increasing lip service to the idea of "sex education," there is very little candid or useful presentation of many of the important facts. Thus a survey made a few years ago showed that only some 50 per cent of married women had any accurate idea of what was the fertile phase of their cycle.

Unlike certain other forms of human activity, the sexual act has—or may have—a rather weighty aftermath. Pregnancy and birth result in the creation of a third human being and therefore involve moral, social, and legal consequences. It certainly should not be undertaken casually or thoughtlessly. For a variety of good reasons which may vary from couple to couple, a majority would prefer to have fewer children than would come into existence as a result of wholly unhampered sexual activity. Sometimes one or another set of circumstances arises which may forbid undertaking another pregnancy at least for a time. This may at once pose the problem of either utilizing a birth control method or abstaining from lovemaking. The choice here is clear, but despite the frequency with which it must be made, not many possess enough facts to form their own opinion. Even the couple who are willing to undertake the responsibilities towards all the children that nature will grant them can profit by familiarizing themselves with some of the relevant facts. It may be of some value to them, for example, to know how many children they may anticipate or what the spacing between them might turn out to be.

It has repeatedly been demonstrated that most American couples at one time or another use some form of birth control. This is done so as to insure that each new arrival in the family unit can be properly cared for, reared, and educated. Most often the choice of the number of children to have is dictated by a conscious or unconscious assessment of the emotional and physical as well as financial reserves. Many couples feel quite justified in taking the position that they may be unable to relate with complete success to the dozen or more children a bountiful nature could bestow on them. Whatever the family goals may be, it is clear that the area of reproduction should not be a twilight zone or, as the doctor so often finds it, an area of jumbled half-truths, myths, and blanks. There is everything to be gained and nothing to be lost from a clear knowledge of the facts. If they aren't taught in school, then they must be sought elsewhere. Certainly the defects of the educational system in this respect or the distorted views that prevail in some segments of society should not predominate. Nor will this kind of knowledge interfere with the esthetics of the relationships between the sexes or the emotions that are felt. The knowledge of how the engine and transmission of an auto work in no way interferes with the enjoyment of a motor trip.

Many newly married couples—and some older ones too —turn to the doctor for basic information. This is as it should be, though sometimes the doctor himself may be surprised at the elementary nature of some of these queries. Sometimes he comes to feel that what should be common knowledge is indeed most uncommon. He often comes to the conclusion that somewhere along the line some parents flub their educational duty. He may sometimes be startled by the discrepancy between formal education and sexual ignorance. But whatever mixture of feelings and ideas he may have, he may not and cannot be derelict in his duty as others have been. He has seen too often the consequence of lack of knowledge in this area, the unwanted pregnancy, the young woman seeking out an abortionist, the exhausted wife who has had five children in rapid succession and is becoming frigid because of the possibility of a sixth pregnancy.

Only a few of the situations he encounters are necessarily desperate or dramatic. A majority of those coming to him are happily married couples content to have a sensible number of children, to love them, and to rear them. All they will want to know is reasonably prudent ways of spacing the offspring, and how this can be done without dreary abstinence or complicated, haphazard, or dangerous methods. A sample of the kinds of questions he hears at one time or another runs something like this:

Q—I am about to get married. If I don't use contraceptives, how long will it be before I get pregnant?

A—On average, about half of all couples can expect that pregnancy will occur within the first six months of

marriage. By the end of a year, approximately 85 per
cent will have achieved pregnancy.

Q—Is there a relationship between frequency of intercourse
and the chances of pregnancy?

A—The chances of becoming pregnant are materially increased when intercourse without the use of contraceptives occurs as often as three times a week. It takes
about twice as long to get pregnant if intercourse occurs
less than twice a week, as compared with an intercourse
frequency of three or more times a week. One study
relating frequency of intercourse to first conception revealed the following relationship:

AVERAGE FREQUENCY OF INTERCOURSE (PER WEEK)	AVERAGE TIME OF FIRST CONCEPTION
Less than 2 times	11.0 months
2 to 2½ times	7.1 "
3 or more times	6.6 "

Another study, reported from the New York Hospital, also
showed that the chance of getting pregnant within a six-
month period was directly related to frequency of intercourse, but yielded even more precise figures:

AVERAGE FREQUENCY OF INTERCOURSE (PER WEEK)	PERCENTAGE OF PREGNANCIES WITHIN 6 MONTHS
All cases (428)	48.4 per cent
Less than 1 time	16.7 " "
More than 1, less than 2 times	32.1 " "
More than 2, less than 3 times	46.3 " "
More than 3, less than 4 times	51.0 " "
4 or more times	83.3 " "

Sex, Fertility, and Birth Control

For many couples, therefore, the chances of pregnancy within a half-year period may almost double if the frequency of intercourse is doubled. Moreover, the chances of pregnancy are still further improved if the frequency of intercourse is increased at around the time of maximum fertility (Chapter 4).

Q—If I continue to refrain from using birth control measures, when will I have my second and third pregnancies?

A—The chances of becoming pregnant are temporarily diminished after a delivery, especially if the baby is nursed. It is true that a few women become pregnant as early as three or four months after delivery, and the likelihood of pregnancy is increased if regular menstrual periods are re-established. Regular menstrual cycles are generally (though not always) delayed so long as the baby is nursed. Here again the probability of a second or third pregnancy also must be related to frequency of intercourse. This is indicated by the following figures:

FREQUENCY OF INTERCOURSE (PER WEEK)	INTERVAL TO 2ND AND 3RD PREGNANCIES
Less than 2 times	21.7 months
Less than 2½ times	19.8 "
3 or more times	12.9 "

Another way of looking at these figures, is as follows: A healthy young couple having intercourse approximately every other day can expect the first pregnancy to occur by six months and the second about one year after the birth of the first baby. Hence by the end of the first three years of marriage there will be two children, and by the end of the first five years of marriage, three.

Q—How many children will I have if I use no birth control measures at all—ever?

A—Fertility tends to diminish with age. This decline with aging is related to multiple other factors, such as frequency of intercourse, fertility of individual cycles, and the like. The probability of becoming pregnant is considerably higher in the decade between twenty and thirty than in the decade between thirty and forty. Of the women in the forty to forty-four group, about half are unable to get pregnant. Remember, too, that a small percentage of women are altogether unable to get pregnant. A still smaller percentage, having gotten pregnant once or twice, fail to conceive thereafter. However, such women form only a small part of the total. In one large group of women of proven fertility, a range of two to sixteen pregnancies was found. *There was an average of 9.8 labors per mother.* So the best estimate would be that you would have upwards of nine children if you married at age twenty and used no birth control measures. In the study referred to, the average interval between pregnancies was 13.3 months, and more than half the women had a delivery every two years.

Q—How do I know whether I am of high, medium, or low fertility?

A—The trouble with all statistics is that they can never be applied accurately to any particular person. It is entirely possible that you may have only two or three pregnancies even though your husband is young and virile and you never use contraceptives. It is even possible that yours may turn out to be one of the 10 per cent of all marriages which are sterile. However, if you are in good health and with reasonably regular periods, you had better go on the assumption that the statistics do hold for you and that you might readily have as many as nine children, and more than nine pregnancies, since statistically about one in five pregnancies may end in a spontaneous miscarriage.

Sex, Fertility, and Birth Control

Q—Is there a falling off in fertility with men, as with women?

A—Aging has far less effect on male reproductive performance than on a woman's. For example, there is no appreciable drop-off in sperm production by males through the twenty-to-forty-five age bracket, the period of the most energetic male reproductive performance. In contrast, there is a decline in the fertility of women past the age of thirty to thirty-five which becomes quite marked after the age of forty. Males in their fifties and sixties are quite capable of becoming fathers, though maternity in this age group is zero. However, one of the limiting factors with the aging male is the diminished capacity for intercourse. The average male in his fifties is down to an intercourse rate of not much more than once a week, which greatly reduces the possibility of pregnancy even if his wife is young and fertile.

Q—Women of two or three generations ago, like my grandmother and great-grandmother, had very large families. Is fertility in women decreasing?

A—There is no reason to believe there has been any change in female fertility in recent generations. All of the apparent marked decrease is due to such factors as later marriage and the use of contraception. The fact of the matter is that in the United States the national birth rate has been declining since 1810. The census figures prove this. From them one can calculate the number of children under age five per thousand women age twenty to forty-four. As Raymond Pearl has shown, the figures come out as follows:

1810	1,358 children
1840	1,085 "
1880	780 "
1920	604 "
1940	419 "
1950	587 "

By this method of calculation, there are less than half as many children per woman of reproductive age at the middle of the twentieth century, as there were at the beginning of the nineteenth century. Economic factors, such as the Great Depression of the 1930's, have undoubtedly played a part—many persons postponed marriage and some did not marry at all. Obviously many who got married also practised contraception, for the birth rate showed a marked decline during that period. Thus in the United States the figures for births per thousand women age fifteen to forty-four were as follows:

1910	126.8
1920	117.9
1930	89.2
1940	79.9
1950	106.2

A comparable drop in the birth rate is true of all countries in the past one hundred years. The large family of the pioneer days seems to have gone out of fashion.

Q—Am I to assume that married couples with small families are practicing contraception?

A—Of course, any particular family you have in mind may be a family unit with limited fertility. However, in the United States, contraception is very widespread among married people. In one 1960 study, 93 per cent of all couples married fifteen years or more were shown to have used some kind of birth control. This held for different religious groups: 95 per cent of all Jewish couples, 84 per cent of all Protestant couples, 70 per cent of all Roman Catholic couples. It is reasonable to suppose, therefore, that any particular married couple will sooner or later be using a contraceptive device or technique. Despite such widespread acceptance and practice, there is still a conspiracy of silence directed against many aspects of control of reproduction—as witness some archaic state laws which up until very recently forbade the dissemination of any information on contraceptives, and even carried penalties directed against doctors who prescribed such devices.

Q—Is there any risk to using a contraceptive device, such as the ones being placed into the uterus?

A—Most of the intrauterine devices are made of plastic. There is no evidence that this plastic has any significant injurious or inflammatory effect. Of course, the fact that the lining in contact with the plastic is shed each month makes it probable that of all the organs in the body, the uterus would be the least likely to have a problem with such an inlying device.

Q—Does the use of contraceptives for a period of time interfere with fertility?

A—There have been numerous studies that clearly indicate that women who use a contraceptive device have no subsequent impairment of fertility. A wife who stops using a diaphragm or foam or any other standard agent has just the same chance of getting pregnant as if she had never used such a device at all. There is some evidence that with women who stop using birth control pills, fertility may even be increased. This is indicated by the fact that pregnancy often occurs quite soon after pills are discontinued, plus the fact that statistically there seems to be a somewhat higher incidence of twins in women who have gone off the pill.

Q—Is it possible for a diaphragm to get lost inside me?

A—Even the slightest knowledge of the anatomy of this area would make clear the impossibility of such an event. In ordinary circumstances the vagina can be regarded as a collapsed pocket whose far end is closed. It is not a canal which is open fore and aft. Hence a device like a diaphragm cannot be inserted into the vagina and disappear into the body's interior. (See Chapter 2.)

Q—How can I get an intrauterine contraceptive device?
A—This device has to be inserted by a doctor. Although the insertion is technically not difficult, it should be done by someone with a background in this subject, such as a specialist in obstetrics and gynecology. Once a device is in (apart from a few that are expelled), it may be counted on to remain in place month after month. There are as yet no guidelines as to whether any of these devices should be replaced, and if so, at what intervals.

Q—What contraceptive method is most suitable for a newlywed?
A—In many respects the pill would be the best. It is the most "natural" in the sense that no contrivances or paraphernalia are needed, and unlike the barriers, such as the condom, it allows for complete physical intimacy. However, the pills have to be started on the fifth day of the menstrual cycle (Chapter 7), so some planning ahead may be necessary. If this has not been done, as when a couple suddenly decide to get married, probably the use of a condom by the groom may be the simplest and most effective approach. After the honeymoon, one of the many methods whose pros and cons are discussed in various chapters may be deemed the most suitable.

Q—Can anything be done to postpone menstruation on a honeymoon?
A—One of the real advantages of the birth control pills is that they can be used to prolong the cycle and postpone menstruation. If it appears that menstruation may occur

on the honeymoon, and if it is desirable to avoid this, taking the pill can be continued past the twentieth day, as is usually recommended in the accompanying instructions. Thus instead of taking the pill for twenty days, the bride-to-be can take it for a longer time, say for thirty days, again with the expectation that a few days after she stops, a period will result. With most of the older pills, this means continuing to take the tablets simply by going on to the next packet. With the more recent sequential pills, in which the last five pills are different from the first fifteen, it would be best to consult the doctor for explicit directions on how the period can be postponed.

The point to be understood is that the dispensing packet for the pills has been arranged to duplicate "the normal twenty-eight" cycle. However, there is nothing specifically desirable about a twenty-eight day cycle— as witness the women who have thirty-three to thirty-five day cycles and who are in excellent health and quite fertile. The fact is that the pills can be taken for thirty days, and if they are then stopped, a thirty-two to thirty-three day cycle will generally result. Or they can be taken for, say, thirty-seven days, which will result in approximately a forty-day cycle. In short, the pills in essence produce an artificial cycle whose duration can be altered at will and at the convenience of the user.

Q—I understand that there is no absolutely reliable birth control method. Is this true?

A—Of the many methods of contraception, no single one has been reported to be always and forever 100 per cent effective. Occasional pregnancies are reported even with the two most reliable methods, the pill and the intrauterine contraceptive device (IUCD). Insofar as the pill is concerned, the problem seems to be that women occcasionally fail to remember that it is a *daily* pill, so that the rare unplanned pregnancy in users of birth control pills has been traced to human error—forgetting to follow instructions. With the next most reliable device, the IUCD, most of the pregnancies have occurred following an unnoted expulsion of the device. When the device has been used for a year or more, following which time unnoted expulsions are quite rare, the unplanned pregnancy rate is of a very low order. With such a device, there is no human error since there is nothing that even a forgetful woman has to remember, no special directions she has to follow. In a large number of women who have retained the device for more than a year, the pregnancy rate is 1.8 per 100 woman years, which translates out to less than 1/40th the expected pregnancy rate had no device been used at all. It is important to remember that many of the reported statistics on the use of one birth control method or another—such as the foam, the condom, or the diaphragm—represent pooled figures, observations on a large number of women, some well motivated, some poorly motivated, some careful about following directions, others careless. Thus with a barrier device, such as the diaphragm or condom, a careful, well-motivated woman or man can count on a high, though not absolute, protection against an unplanned pregnancy. Even better results are secured by combining methods, as, for example, the use of both foam and condom until three days after the temperature curve indicates that the time of fertility has passed (see Chapter 10).

Q—Is the choice of contraceptives affected by frequency of intercourse?

A—To a certain extent, yes. The chances of becoming pregnant are considerably increased by frequent intercourse, and this may have to be considered in making a choice of contraceptive. As discussed earlier in this chapter, the chances of a wife becoming pregnant are greatly increased if intercourse is three or more times a week as compared to once a week. When intercourse occurs no more frequently than once a week, the possibility of pregnancy drops off considerably; in fact such a low rate of intercourse is one cause for sterile marriages. When intercourse is that infrequent, it may not be considered advisable for a woman to take a daily birth control pill. Since the long-range effects of the pill are unknown, it hardly seems reasonable to undergo whatever risk (if any) is attached to its use when the over-all chances of pregnancy are slight. Various local methods of contraception, such as foam or cream (with or without a condom), would seem to be riskfree and therefore preferable.

If intercourse occurs three or more times per week, however, the pregnancy rate soars and hence an efficient contraceptive method is desirable. Here the pill or the IUCD might be the best answer because of its proven high efficiency and as a method of avoiding an otherwise almost daily need for creams, jellies, diaphragms, or other day-in, day-out paraphernalia and maneuvers. Some couples object to the need for such frequently repeated procedures. In addition, the theoretical inadequacy of a particular contraceptive would be increased. For example, if the method of contraception is a condom, intercourse once a week means fifty-two condoms per year, whereas intercourse four or more times a week means 200 to 250 condoms per year. Hence the risk of using a defective condom or one that breaks obviously goes up. Factors such as this should be weighed in the choice of a contraceptive. Not that frequency of intercourse is the sole decisive factor. Contrast for example, a young passionate couple having frequent intercourse but willing to accept the possibility of pregnancy with an older less passionate couple who are completely unreceptive to the idea of another pregnancy. For both these couples the dominant factor in selecting a contraceptive may be their attitude towards having a further addition to the family. Where pregnancy is risky or dangerous to the woman, the most effective method should be sought out, even if the frequency of intercourse rate is low.

Some Frequent Questions About the Pill

Q—How does the birth control pill work?

A—There seem to be two principal modes of action. The chief one is interference with the normal course of events in the ovary which ordinarily would result in an egg being produced during each menstrual cycle. Women who take the pill fail to produce an egg, hence are infertile. A second effect seems to be on the mucous secretion of the cervix. This is rendered thicker and less permeable. It is therefore more resistant to penetration and movement on the part of the sperm cell.

Q—If as a result of taking the pills for several years I fail to conceive, is there any danger that this might continue when I stop the pill and try to get pregnant?

A—Absolutely not. There is abundant evidence that once a woman who has been taking the pills discontinues them, her fertility and her capacity to become pregnant promptly return. It is important to bear in mind that one of the original uses of the pill was to increase fertility in marriages which were sterile because the woman's function was subpar.

Q—Is the birth control pill licit for the Roman Catholic couple?

A—The birth control pill can be used by any Roman Catholic woman as a medication against sterility or to regularize the cycle. At present it cannot be used as a birth control measure, since the only method of birth control sanctioned by the Church is the rhythm method (Chapter 11). At the time of the Ecumenical Council, there was a good deal of discussion of the possibility that the birth control pill might be ruled licit for family planning by Roman Catholics. This did not turn out to be the case.

Q—Can the birth control pill kill off an early embryo or damage it if taken without knowledge of the pregnancy?

A—If a woman who is already in the early stages of pregnancy takes a birth control pill, there is no interference with the progress of the pregnancy. Birth control pills neither kill off an early embryo nor produce miscarriages. In the currently used dosages, they do not have any masculinizing or other effect on an early embryo if one is developing unbeknownst to the pill taker.

Q—Is the pill a dangerous or risky birth control method?

A—Despite the discussions that have come up from time to time, it can be flatly stated that so far as is known after a great deal of accumulated experience the pills are safe. The question as to whether there may be more clotting in the veins or complications with such clots for the pill taker has been difficult to answer in a final and definitive manner. Women had spontaneously experienced clotting in veins, sometimes with severe complications, long before the pills were invented. The best evidence available at present indicates that such clotting is not increased in pill takers. Nor is there any evidence that tumors in the reproductive tract have increased in women taking the pill. Indeed, in one large group of women whose experiences were followed for more than eight years, certain common tumors seem to have decreased below the expected level. (For a more detailed discussion of this and related points, see Chapter 7.)

Q—Are there some women who should not take the pills?
A—Yes, there are. Women who should not take the pills are the following:
1. Any woman who has had a history of cancer of the reproductive tract or of the breast.
2. Any woman who has large or significant fibroids. (These are benign tumors of the uterus.)
3. Any woman who has had a past history of phlebitis or clotting in veins. It is not known whether this precaution is really justified, but current medical practice adheres to it for the time being.
4. Very young women—those in their early or mid-teens —should not take the pill. In them the pill may interfere with possible further bone growth.
5. There are a few medical conditions, such as migraine, diabetes, and epilepsy, which may conceivably be aggravated by the pills. If contraception is considered desirable, there need not be any hesitation or fear; there is no harm in trying the pills even when such conditions exist. Only a minority of women with these illnesses experience any adverse effect from the pill.

Q—Will the pills make me gain weight?
A—Some weight gain was reported by women taking the early versions of the pill. This seems to have decreased considerably with the more recent types, and the most recent studies indicate little or no significant weight gain. Some of the weight gain reported is due to the fluid accumulation which normally occurs during the menstrual cycle and pregnancy. This is not a true weight gain in the sense of an accumulation of fat.

Sex, Fertility, and Birth Control

Q—Does the pill produce any discomfort?

A—The overwhelming majority of women have no difficulty at all with the pill and are aware of no discomfort when taking it. A few have complained of mild nausea, particularly during the first two or three months of pill-taking. This tends to subside after a few cycles. It seems to resemble the nausea encountered in pregnancy and may be decreased or obviated by taking the pill after the evening meal or on retiring.

Q—Are there any psychological effects from taking the pill?

A—A few women have complained of feeling "off" or of being somewhat depressed while on a particular pill. Again, this seems to resemble some of the feelings complained of by women towards the end of a normal cycle, sometimes described as "premenstrual tension." If this does occur, a shift to another pill may be indicated as the effect seems to vary from one pill to another. In general, most women notice no psychological effects one way or another. Sexual drive seems to be in the main unaltered; a few women report decreased sexual interest, others increased sexual interest. The latter may well be due to lifting of the fear of pregnancy, a fear which often plays some part in diminishing a woman's sexual drive.

Q—What can be done for breast tenderness while taking the pill?

A—The various birth control pills available currently differ with respect to this. If breast tenderness is persistent or annoying, a shift to another pill may be advisable.

Q—If after taking the pills according to directions no menstrual period follows, what should be done?

A—Skipping of a period is not unusual with some of the

present birth control pills. It is more frequently encountered in women who have noted that their period has become scantier once they are on the pill. After a succession of such scanty periods, a period may be skipped altogether. No particular significance need be attached to this. If menstruation does not occur as expected, the pill should be resumed no later than the seventh day after the last one was taken. It is sometimes desirable to shift to another pill. Some of the newer sequential pills produce rather longer and more abundant menstrual periods.

Q—Can I start off on any day of the month with the pills and count on not getting pregnant?

A—Emphatically not. The pills must be taken sufficiently early in the cycle to head off the growth phase in the ovary which leads to formation of an egg. It is for this reason that they have to be started on the fifth day after the beginning of the menstrual period. A woman who starts taking the pill, say, on the tenth day of her cycle, would be very likely to go ahead and ovulate— and thus be fertile during that cycle.

Q—There seem to be a number of pills available. Which one is the most suitable?

A—There are indeed a considerable number of birth control pills on the market at present, varying somewhat in the amount of hormones they contain. Some are mixtures of hormones, others not. They all seem to be equally effective in serving their prime function, which is to prevent pregnancy. The doctor will choose the pill with which he is perhaps most familiar or which he deems best for a particular patient. The doctor may be aware that some pills produce scantier menstrual periods than others. He may choose such a one for a woman with a history of painful, long periods. Occasionally, a woman who may have spotting and staining while taking one of the pills (breakthrough bleeding—see Chapter 7) may escape this annoyance with a shift to another pill. New versions, with modifications which may be superior, have appeared in the past few years. Hence a shift from one pill to another may be desirable for everyone involved and is sometimes recommended by the manufacturers themselves.

Q—Should not the pills be sold freely in the drug store rather than only on a doctor's prescription?

A—As has been noted above, some women should not take the pill for sound medical reasons. Only your doctor is able to pass judgment on whether or not this holds true for you. Thus if your doctor knew that you had slowly growing fibroid tumors of the uterus, he might hesitate to have you start on the pills and risk the increase in rate of growth of these tumors that might occur. Also, since there is a multiplicity of pills which do vary somewhat, one of them might be best for a specific patient. Only the doctor has the professional judgment to make this choice. Once your doctor has selected a pill for you, he can give the druggist permission to renew the medication on request for a considerable, though not indefinite, period of time. Until the long-term safety of the pill is unequivocally established, your doctor may not want you to have automatic renewal of the pill year after year without his giving you a physical check-up, particularly of the reproductive tract, at reasonable intervals.

Q—Has taking the pills for a number of years had any effect on a subsequent pregnancy?

A—No. Neither the baby nor any aspect of the subsequent pregnancy is in any way affected by previous consumption of birth control pills.

Q—Does taking of the pill postpone the menopause ("change of life")?

A—One of the idle speculations bandied about when the pills were first distributed raised this possibility. Experience with the pills indicates, however, that they have no effect on the menopause. The menopause appears in due time, just as it would have had the pills not been used. Use of the pills for controlling some of the symptoms of menopause, such as the uncomfortable flushes and sweats, has been advocated. They are in fact very efficient in this respect.

2.
The Anatomy of the Sexes

Tʜᴇ sᴛᴏʀʏ ɪs ᴛᴏʟᴅ of the girl in the freshman biology class who turned to her partner and murmured, "I just love the idea of there being two sexes, don't you?"

Whether she was expressing amazement, wonder, or delight, or perhaps all three emotions, all of us can surely understand and appreciate the positiveness of her response. For in every respect the sexes are indeed wonderfully different; and the sex organs—male and female both—remarkably and uniquely constructed. Moreover, it is natural for the normal human being to take pleasure in this.

For all of the complexity of human emotions, particularly of love between man and and woman, it is really the sex organs that form the physical basis for what someone has termed, rather pedantically, "the positive feelings which spring up between individuals of the same species but of different sexes." From the biologic point of view it is the sex organs, too, that guarantee each of us the experience of relating positively to some other person. For while it is perfectly possible to sit thinking deep thoughts in solitude, or digest a fine meal in privacy, reproductive functioning cannot take place except with someone else—someone of the opposite sex.

To further insure her mating designs, nature has endowed the sexual organs with specially fabricated nerve endings. These are quite unlike the nerve endings to be found anywhere else in the skin and are therefore referred to as the genital corpuscles. It is these corpuscles that transmit the unique forms of sensation associated with sexual reactions. In the male, these special sensory endings are distributed over the penis, particularly over its soft tip and the undersurface of the shaft. In the female, they center mainly in the clitoris, with the breasts, particularly the nipples, forming what is termed a secondary erogenous zone.

But except for these tiny nerve endings shared in common, there is little in the way of anatomical structure that is the same in both sexes. Rather, sexual characteristics are a matter of contrasts. Thus the penis of the male is an organ of penetration, the vagina of the female a canal. The testes or sex glands of the male produce sperm in huge amounts, while the ovaries, the comparable female organs, turn out relatively very few eggs. Indeed, whereas in the female all twenty-eight days of a menstrual cycle are concerned with the building up of a single egg in the hope that this will be fertilized, the male each day produces sperm by the million. Also, as we shall see later on, one might say that whereas the female in her egg production concentrates on quality, the male concentrates on quantity. Biologically, there are many perfectly good reasons why this should be so, and to know these reasons is important. It helps us understand the functioning of our bodies—sometimes even, to some extent, the functioning of our emotions.

Sex, Fertility, and Birth Control

The Male Anatomy

The reproductive organs of the male consist of the penis and the testicles, which are the repositories of the sperm. The quantity of sperm produced by the mature male reaches stupendous totals in a lifetime. The average semen specimen delivered at the time of orgasm is about a teaspoonful in volume. The number of sperm will vary considerably from one man to another, but certainly two hundred million would be a pretty fair average. Thus the sperm in any single ejaculate can theoretically fertilize a number of eggs corresponding to the entire living population of the United States. A healthy male can produce this number of sperm daily, or at least several times a week. His lifetime total reaches incomprehensible, astronomical figures. Thus the sperm production of one vigorous man could within a few weeks—or at most months—be sufficient to father all the human beings that have ever trod the surface of the earth.

The huge number of sperm furnished with each ejaculate points up the minuteness of these strange little cells, especially when one realizes that much of the ejaculate consists of fluids furnished by the prostate and the seminal vesicles, secretions which are free of sperm. Hence the actual volume of the sperm themselves is only a small part of the total volume of the ejaculate. The biologist Carl G. Hartman has estimated that one third of a stick of chewing gum, formed into a small ball, would correspond to the volume of the three billion sperm cells necessary to father the world's present population: this mass of sperm cells is about the size of a pepper corn.

Testicles

This prodigious manufacture of sperm cells begins at around the time of puberty and goes on for sixty to seventy years, or even longer. (Males in their seventies can become

SECTION OF THE MALE PELVIS

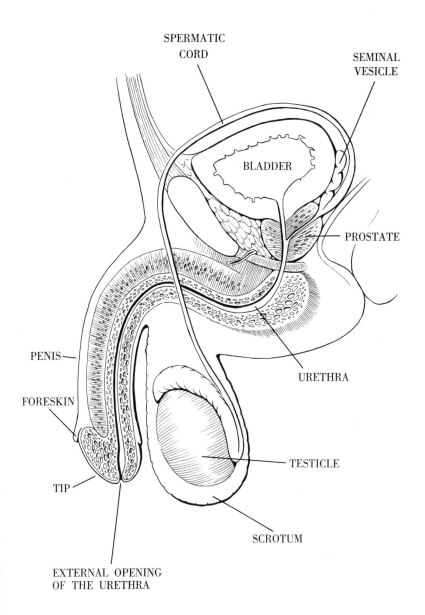

FIGURE 1

fathers. The limiting factor is their power of erection, not the presence of sperm.) The sperm-manufacturing organs are the testicles, also known as the testes. It is in some ways surprising that these vital and important organs should be externally situated and therefore vulnerable to blows or other forms of damage. On the other hand, as we shall see, nature had a good reason for such an arrangement.

The testicles are located in the scrotum, a pouch of skin which hangs down between the thighs. They can be readily felt as two firm ovoid balls, each some two inches in length, and perhaps an inch in diameter. The basic element of structure in the testis is a delicate filament-like tubule called the spermatic tubule. There are many miles of spermatic tubules in each testis, much as a ball of yarn is composed of hundreds of feet of wool. The spermatic tubule can be likened to a microscopic canal. Along the banks of the canal sperm manufacture is constantly going on, and the finished product, the sperm, move out and into the canal much as logs may be floated from a forest down river.

The finished sperm cell is a streamlined unit designed with only one end in mind: to seek out and fertilize the egg. In the manufacturing process that creates the sperm cell, large round lining cells are transformed into slender tailed elements (Fig. 2). A human sperm cell can be compared to a tadpole with its large round head and slender vibratile tail. The head is packed with all the hereditary characteristics bequeathed by the father. The lashing movements of the tail are what propel the cell forward at the rate of perhaps an inch an hour. Thus the sperm cell can be regarded as a little packet of heredity with a built-in mechanism for delivering the package.

Although newly formed sperm are indistinguishable from those found in the semen ejaculated at the time of intercourse, they are immature and not yet ready for functioning. Sperm cells freshly removed from a testicle are not

CROSS-SECTION OF THE TESTICLE AND ADJACENT DUCTS

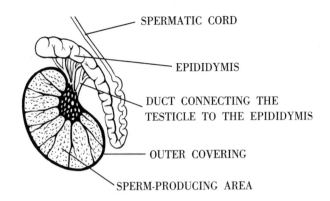

SPERMATIC CORD

EPIDIDYMIS

DUCT CONNECTING THE
TESTICLE TO THE EPIDIDYMIS

OUTER COVERING

SPERM-PRODUCING AREA

SCHEMATIC DRAWING OF THE TESTICLE
Arrows show sperm pathway

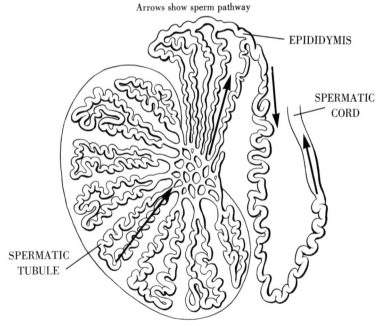

EPIDIDYMIS

SPERMATIC
CORD

SPERMATIC
TUBULE

FIGURE 2

SPERM PRODUCTION
(Greatly enlarged cross-section of a spermatic tubule)

The sequence of events that trans-
forms the lining cells into sperm
cells is indicated by arrows.

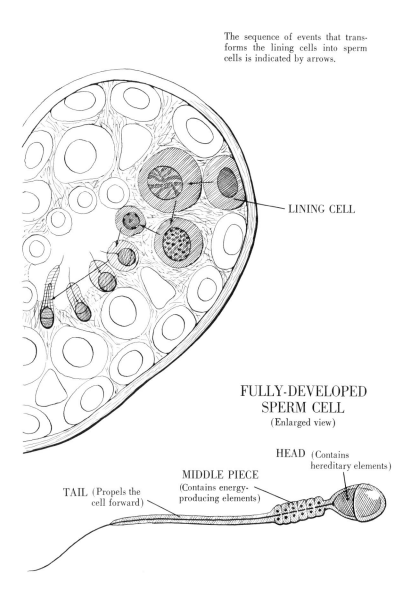

LINING CELL

FULLY-DEVELOPED
SPERM CELL
(Enlarged view)

HEAD (Contains
hereditary elements)

MIDDLE PIECE
(Contains energy-
producing elements)

TAIL (Propels the
cell forward)

FIGURE 3

SPERM PATHWAY FROM
TESTICLE TO THE EXTERNAL WORLD

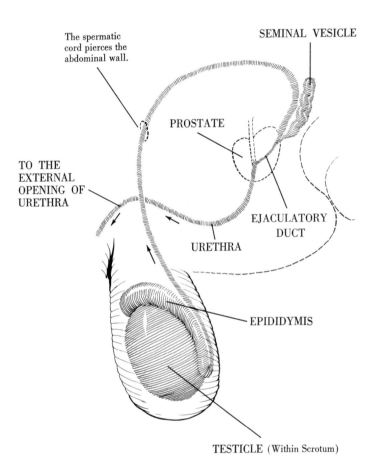

The arrows indicate the direction of the pathway of
the sperm from the testicle to the external opening
of the urethra at the tip of the penis.

FIGURE 4

"ripe" and not capable of fertilizing an egg. They mature as they slowly make their way out of the fine canals of the testis into larger ducts. One of the way stations on this outward journey is in a thickened area known as the epididymis, which sits atop each testis. From here the sperm move on upwards through a wider canal termed the spermatic cord, a kind of ropelike structure from which the testis appears to hang. The spermatic cord runs up and out of the scrotum over the brim of the pelvic bone, pierces the abdominal wall at this point, and enters into the pelvis. Within the pelvis and in close conjunction to the prostate gland and the seminal vesicles, the final pathway for the sperm becomes a system of fine ducts, the ejaculatory ducts. The ejaculatory ducts empty into the urethra; and from the urethra, which is the major channel running through the penis, a pathway to the external world is furnished.

It is clear that because of the position of the testes the sperm must go on a long roundabout route before they emerge from the urethra. Would it not have made more sense to have the testicles, like the ovaries, located in the interior of the body where they would be safe from blows and injuries? Would it not be more reasonable to have them located along with the prostate at the base of the penis, and bypass the need for a long spermatic cord?

The answer to these questions seems to be in the fact that sperm production cannot go on at body temperature. In the condition known as undescended testicle, in which the organ is retained within the pelvis, no sperm production occurs. Furthermore, if insulating material is wrapped around the testicles so that the temperature within the scrotum rises to that of the body, sperm production either falters or ceases altogether. In fact, the need for maintaining the testicles at less than body temperature accounts for the peculiar thermal sensitivity of the scrotum.

Unlike ordinary skin, the scrotum has muscle fibers within it which control the size of the pouch. Cold makes

POSITIONS OF THE SCROTUM

RELAXED SCROTUM

Muscle fibers surrounding the testicle and spermatic cord relax when warm.

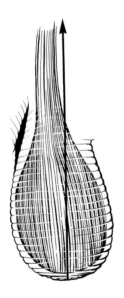

CONTRACTED SCROTUM

Cold causes the muscle fibers to contract. The testicle is drawn up towards the body and the excess scrotal skin becomes wrinkled.

FIGURE 5

THE PROSTATE AND SEMINAL VESICLES
(Viewed from behind)

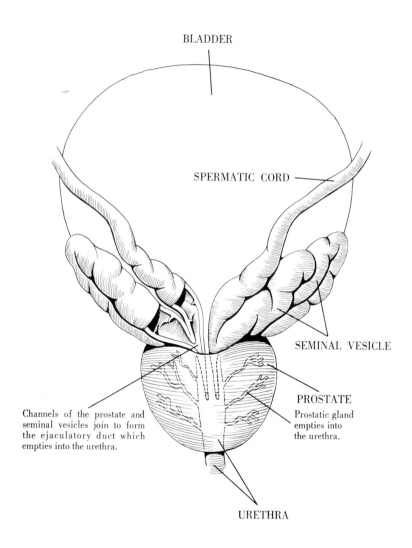

BLADDER

SPERMATIC CORD

SEMINAL VESICLE

PROSTATE

Prostatic gland
empties into
the urethra.

Channels of the prostate and
seminal vesicles join to form
the ejaculatory duct which
empties into the urethra.

URETHRA

FIGURE 6

these muscle fibers contract so that the scrotum brings the testicles up towards the groin in an obvious attempt to warm them. At such times the scrotum may assume a thickened, wrinkled, or corrugated appearance. Exposure to warmth on the other hand, as in hot weather, may produce a great relaxation of the scrotum which then hangs low, appears thin and stretched out, with the testicles at their maximum distance from the trunk. (There is one exception to this: during intercourse, especially near the time of orgasm, the testes are brought up close to the base of the penis.) The harmful effects of elevated temperature can be observed in some conditions in which there is fever. If prolonged, marked reduction in sperm formation will occur.

The prostate and seminal vesicles are two accessory glands which contribute fluid secretions to the semen. Although these secretions are known not to be absolutely necessary to reproduction by the male, they do form the bulk of the ejaculated material. The prostate is a gland about the size and appearance of a chestnut. It is located at the base of the sperm's final channel, the urethra, and therefore quite close to the bladder opening. (It is this unfortunate location that is responsible for the obstruction of urinary flow which sometimes occurs in the later years, since the prostate commonly enlarges in the aging male.) Prostatic secretion is an opaque, whitish fluid of milklike appearance and consistency. The seminal vesicles are two slender sacs located just to each side of the prostate. Contrary to some older ideas, no sperm are found in the seminal vesicles. Their secretion consists of a somewhat thick ropy material which contributes to the viscosity of the semen.

Blending of these secretions with the sperm from the spermatic cord occurs at the time of the orgasm. This blending is not uniform; it has been demonstrated that there is a higher percentage of sperm in the first part of the ejaculate than in the remainder. As has already been said, on average the amount ejaculated is about a teaspoonful. This, however, varies from one male to another. The amount may also be diminished if intercourse is repeated at close intervals.

It is sometimes important to determine the number of sperm furnished by the male—such a count is often the first step in evaluating couples who come to a doctor complaining of childlessness. Sperm counts are done in exactly the same manner as blood cell counts. Most males have a sperm count on the order of 50 to 100 million per cc. (A cc, or cubic centimeter, is about a quarter of a teaspoon.) Sperm cell counts below 50 million are generally associated with low fertility. Actually, low fertility is more common when the sperm count drops below 30 million, although even at this level fatherhood is by no means ruled out. However, when the count falls below 20 million, sterility is the rule; and in some sterile marriages the male may have no sperm whatsoever in the ejaculate. This condition is known as azoospermia. It may not be suspected unless a sperm count is done, since it does not affect a man's ability to have normal erections and intercourse with an apparently normal ejaculate. Another factor that may contribute to lack of fertility is the number of abnormal sperm forms, which is often higher when the sperm count is low. Considering the vast number of sperm constantly being formed, it is not surprising to find abnormal specimens coming off the production line—there is, after all, no inspector sorting out the rejects. Such abnormal sperm appear in various forms: unusually large heads, double heads or double tails, partially fused sperm, and the like. In doing a sperm count, it is therefore customary to make a notation as to the extent to which abnormal forms occur, and also to record observations on the rate of motion and other evidences of activity of the sperm in the sample.

Scattered amongst the spermatic tubules are groups of cells which are not involved in sperm manufacture. They are known as the interstitial cells, and they manufacture male hormone. This hormone is delivered directly into the blood stream and is responsible for such masculine characteristics as the larger size of the muscles and bones, increased amounts of facial and body hair, the pattern of scalp hair, and other masculine characteristics. More importantly, this hormone, known as testosterone, is responsible for the growth of the penis and scrotum as well as the prostate and seminal vesicles.

If testosterone is not furnished in normal amounts at the time of puberty, none of the usual maturation in physique and sexual development occurs. The individual then retains many of the characteristics of the immature boy. A man in whom such sexual characteristics have not developed is sometimes termed a eunuch. The hormone-secreting cells of the testes are themselves in turn controlled by a hormone emanating from the pituitary, a tiny gland at the base of the brain. Hence the failure of sexual maturation in a male may occasionally be traced to a disorder in the pituitary gland. More often it is due to damage to the testes from disease or from a failure to descend from the body cavity into the scrotum.

Since it is the testes that manufacture both sperm and male hormone, they are in fact the glands that make a male a male. Despite this undoubted fact, it is the penis that is more often regarded as the prime organ of male sexuality. This is due to the fact that it is the penis that undergoes dramatic changes in size and appearance as a result of sexual stimulation. In the quiescent state the penis is a soft small organ which hangs downward over the scrotum. Within a few seconds of sexual stimulus—which can be any one of a great number of events, thoughts, or sights— the penis can rapidly increase in size and volume. The organ enlarges to an average length of approximately 5 to 6 inches and moves upwards into a more vertical position. This is the phenomenon known as erection and refers to the fact that the organ sweeps up in an arc from its downward to the upward position.

Erection is due to the peculiar construction of the penis. Its shaft is composed of three cylinders of tissue which are honeycombed with a network of spaces capable of considerable distention. The chain of events that results in erection may be likened to those which occur when a forcibly collapsed sponge is placed in a fluid and the pressure released. As the collapsed spaces of the sponge expand and take up the fluid, the volume and turgidity of the sponge increase. In the stimulated male, a complicated interaction between nerves and blood vessels produces a similar filling up of the shaft of the penis. As a result, the diameter of the penis more than doubles and the soft spongy organ becomes stiff and rigid. The state of firmness is generally maintained as long as the sexually stimulating circumstances are maintained. It usually rapidly reverses itself following orgasm. The tip end of the penis, known as the glans, is composed of a softer, somewhat more yielding tissue, not erectile in its composition. Hence it remains relatively soft during the erection of the organ. The "give" at the tip or penetrating end of the penis obviously facilitates vaginal entry.

Traversing the entire length of the penis, and therefore elongating also during the process of erection, is a tubelike channel called the urethra. This is a channel used in common by the urinary and the reproductive systems. However, in full erection, an interesting mechanism makes it impossible for the bladder to empty itself. Hence urination cannot occur from the erect penis.

At the tip end of the urethra are a few small glands which secrete a small amount of a lubricating fluid. A little of this may exude during stimulation. When sexual stimulation results in orgasm, concerted muscular contractions occur, coordinated by the network of nerves going to the various sexual structures. As a result, sperm from their

LONGITUDINAL SECTION OF THE MALE PELVIS

(Showing location of bladder, prostate, ejaculatory tract)

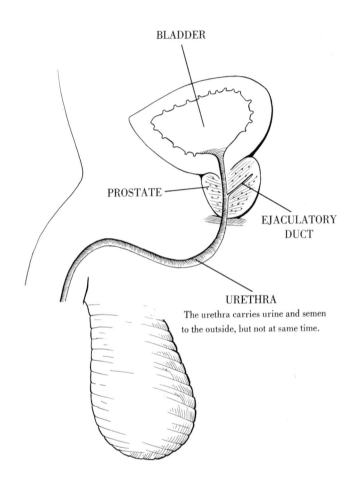

BLADDER

PROSTATE

EJACULATORY
DUCT

URETHRA
The urethra carries urine and semen
to the outside, but not at same time.

FIGURE 7

channel and the secretions from the prostate and seminal vesicles are propelled into the urethra and on out through its opening. These initial contractions are sufficiently propulsive to hurl the semen up to 12 to 24 inches away. Successive contractions are somewhat weaker. Hence the first part of the semen may emerge in spurts and the rest tends to come out in dribbles. Following ejaculation, the penis may remain erect for a short interval, particularly if movement and stimulation are continued. More often a fairly rapid decrease in the character of the erection occurs within a minute or so. Penile size begins to dwindle so that at this point in intercourse the sensation of a loss of contact is felt.

Over a considerable range, the size of the penis, whether in the stimulated or unstimulated state, has no relation to sexual or reproductive performance. The idea (or the fear) some men have that their penis is somewhat smaller than average and therefore will perform less well is not justified in fact. The facts of the matter are that the vagina is a distensible organ whose walls normally are in fairly close contact. The vaginal walls give way in accommodating fashion to the extent determined by the situation. It is this elementary fact that insures the basis for sexual harmony between couples despite the variations in bodily and genital sizes. Hence disproportions of any significance in genital size are quite rare. Insofar as sexual performance is concerned, capacity for intercourse, duration of intercourse, and the potentiality for fatherhood bear no relation to observed fluctuations in penile size.

The Female Anatomy

In contrast with the sexual organs of the male, which are external and plain to see, those of the female are modestly interiorized. In the strict sense, the female has no external generative organs, but rather structures which

THE FEMALE VULVA
(External view)

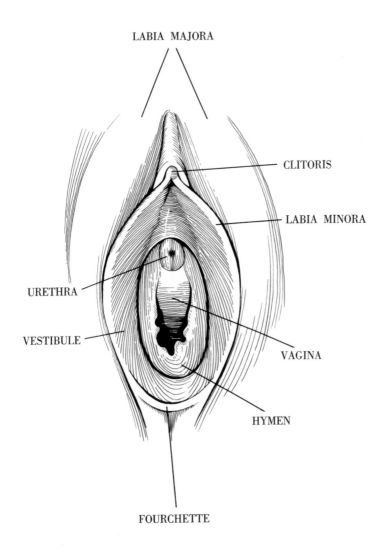

LABIA MAJORA

CLITORIS

LABIA MINORA

URETHRA

VESTIBULE

VAGINA

HYMEN

FOURCHETTE

FIGURE 8

are gateways to the reproductive tract itself. These external anatomical structures are collectively referred to as the vulva. The vulva may be regarded as that space which is bounded by the outer larger folds known as the labia majora (literally, the larger lips). The labia majora are essentially rolled up folds of skin whose substance is made up of fatty tissue. They are covered by curly hair, known as the pubic hair. The pubic hair extends upwards from the labia and characteristically forms a broad relatively straight patch running across the pubic brim. This patch of hair is known as the escutcheon. Its triangular shape is characteristic of the female and is due to the action of the woman's sex hormones.

The two labia minora, or lesser lips, are folds of tissue which are thinner and more delicate than the outer larger ones. They vary somewhat in size, and in some women may appear partially concealed by the larger outer lips. The labia minora are entirely hairless. They form two sides of a triangle at whose top or apex is situated the clitoris, a tiny organ of considerable sensitivity. Below, the labia minora merge into the tissues adjacent to the vagina. The shallow space bounded by the lesser lips is sometimes referred to as the vestibule, in analogy to the entry space of a house. In the vestibule and at the very entrance to the vagina, indeed partially guarding it, is a famous but rather small and variable fold of tissue known as the hymen. The hymen when small may stretch easily and therefore present little or no obstacle to intercourse. More often it may be stretched with first intercourse and undergo superficial tearing, perhaps with light bleeding, an event known as defloration. Sometimes, especially if the hymen is larger or tougher than usual, gentle dilation may be medically advised for an expectant bride. In any event, the presence or absence of a full-blown hymeneal barrier does not constitute proof regarding virginity.

The clitoris is a small structure above the vaginal open-

SECTION OF THE FEMALE PELVIS
(Showing external and internal reproductive structures)

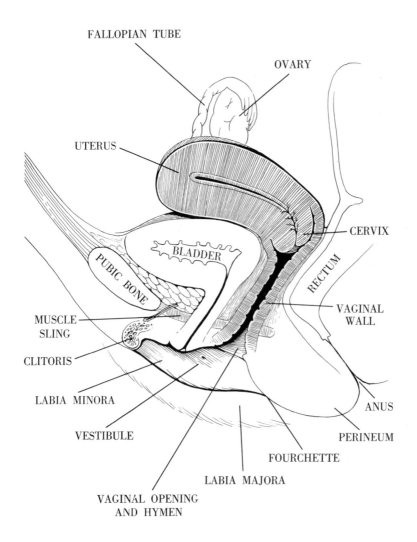

FALLOPIAN TUBE

OVARY

UTERUS

CERVIX

BLADDER

PUBIC BONE

RECTUM

MUSCLE SLING

VAGINAL WALL

CLITORIS

LABIA MINORA

ANUS

VESTIBULE

PERINEUM

FOURCHETTE

LABIA MAJORA

VAGINAL OPENING AND HYMEN

FIGURE 9

ing which can be regarded as a miniaturized penis. Just below it is the opening to the urinary tract, the urethra, which in contrast to the male is separately located in the female. The clitoris, like the penis, is composed of erectile tissue; it too can swell with sexual stimulation. Also like the penis, the clitoris is an erogenous structure, particularly responsive to touch stimulation. In fact, much of the vulvo-vaginal area, the lesser lips, and the vestibule, as well as the clitoris are highly responsive sexually both to foreplay and during intercourse.

Before we examine the rest of the female reproductive tract, it is desirable here to consider the invisible but important muscle tissue in this area. The sling of muscle which extends from the pubic bone in front to the coccyx or tail bone behind is sometimes referred to as the pelvic floor. Portions of this muscle tissue are arranged so as to surround all the openings of structures in the pelvic floor. Such circularly disposed muscle bundles are found around the vagina, the urethra, and the rectum. When they contract, they narrow or pinch off the openings in the same manner as tightening the drawstrings can close the opening of a pouch. A muscle that can thus close down or narrow an opening is called a sphincter. A sphincter of this sort surrounds the vaginal opening. If it tightens up, as it may in anxiety or tension, penetration is more difficult and this may produce pain during intercourse. Conversely, these muscles appear to be more relaxed in the sexually stimulated woman. Involuntary, vigorous repetitive contractions of the muscles of the pelvic floor seem to be an essential element in the climax or orgasm.

Just within the vaginal opening are two glands known as Bartholin's glands. Particularly during sexual stimulation, the glands secrete a lubricating fluid which can facilitate intercourse. The vagina itself is a pouchlike structure some four or five inches in length. The opening of the pouch is at the vulva. Its opposite closed end, sometimes termed the

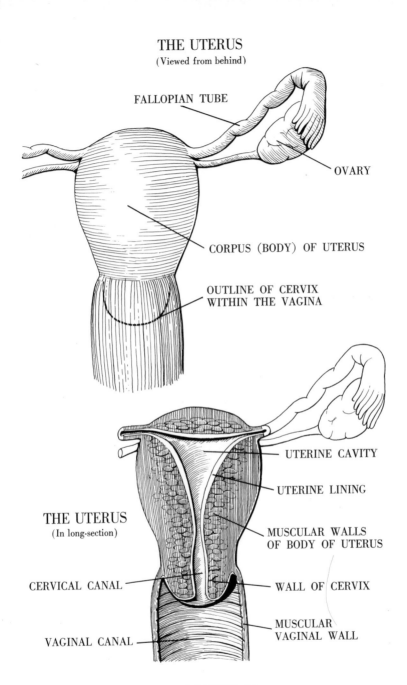

THE UTERUS
(Viewed from behind)

FALLOPIAN TUBE

OVARY

CORPUS (BODY) OF UTERUS

OUTLINE OF CERVIX
WITHIN THE VAGINA

THE UTERUS
(In long-section)

UTERINE CAVITY

UTERINE LINING

MUSCULAR WALLS
OF BODY OF UTERUS

CERVICAL CANAL

WALL OF CERVIX

MUSCULAR
VAGINAL WALL

VAGINAL CANAL

FIGURE 10

vault, encloses the cervix, which is the lowermost portion of the uterus. In most circumstances the vaginal walls are in reasonably close approximation. However, the vagina is capable of a considerable amount of distensibility, something that occurs during intercourse and even more strikingly during the birth of the baby. The vagina has a lining which varies in thickness during a woman's lifetime. Before puberty and after the menopause the lining is thin and delicate. Throughout a woman's reproductive years it is considerably thicker, hence obviously related to her active sexual functioning. In the sexually mature woman the outer cells of the lining are flattened and under the microscope appear as thin, somewhat opaque, saucerlike little elements. They are known as cornified cells.

Cornified cells are of considerable importance, since they appear only when adequate amounts of the female sex hormone known as estrogen are being produced. In fact, the appearance of cornified cells is one of the most sensitive indicators of the action of this female hormone. For this reason they appear in greatest numbers at around midcycle, when the egg cell is ready to be shed and the amount of the female hormone is at its height. Many of the cornified and other cells forming the lining contain a starchlike substance called glycogen. Glycogen can be readily broken down into mildly acidic substances of which the foremost is lactic acid. As a consequence, in the sexually mature woman the vagina is slightly acid in character. This acidity prevents the growth of many harmful bacteria, and it is for this reason that vaginal douches are often acidified with vinegar. It is a curious and apparently parodoxical fact that acidity is also harmful to human sperm.

The uterus (womb) is the organ of pregnancy, the baby's home prior to its birth. In the nonpregnant mature woman it measures approximately three inches in height, two inches in width, and two inches in thickness. In size and shape it is roughly comparable to a pear which has been somewhat flattened. The uterus can be divided into a major portion, called the corpus, and a smaller portion which protrudes into the vagina, known as the cervix. The cervix therefore corresponds to the smaller end of the pear. Corresponding to the stem of the pear is a tiny canal which runs through the cervix and expands into the cavity of the uterus. The opening of the cervical canal is known as the os (*os*, literally mouth). The os usually contains a moderate amount of a mucous secretion. This secretion is thinner and more copious in the interval before ovulation; it is produced by glands which are abundant in this part of the lining. In contrast to the lining higher up, the lining of the cervix goes through no marked changes, nor is it cast off at the time of menstruation.

The Uterine Lining

The uterine lining is remarkable in two ways: 1) It is the nesting area in which the fertilized egg implants and develops into a baby. 2) In the absence of pregnancy it goes through cyclic changes at approximately 28-day intervals.

In the absence of a fertilized egg, much of the lining is sloughed off in the dramatic event known as menstruation. Following menstruation a cycle of growth of a repetitive character again occurs. At the end of menstruation the lining is very low. Some of it is not covered by the usual layer of outer cells but lies exposed, with here and there open blood vessels which are bleeding. The repair of this damaged bleeding surface occurs perhaps more rapidly here than anywhere else in the body. Then, with the increasing level of hormones secreted from the ovary, the lining begins to thicken and its glands multiply and produce increasing amounts of secretion. By the time the fertilized egg arrives, the lining has reached a maximum height of up to three-eighths of an inch and presents a delicate velvety surface.

THE UTERINE LINING

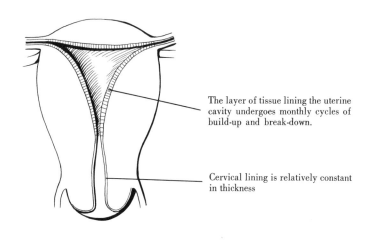

The layer of tissue lining the uterine cavity undergoes monthly cycles of build-up and break-down.

Cervical lining is relatively constant in thickness

THE MENSTRUAL CYCLE

(The appearance of the uterine lining during 1 full cycle)

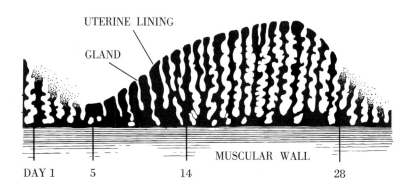

UTERINE LINING

GLAND

MUSCULAR WALL

DAY 1   5   14   28

The cycle begins on the 1st day of bleeding. After bleeding (menstruation) ends, a gradual thickening and gland development begins. This build-up continues to the 28th day if pregnancy does not occur.

FIGURE 11

It is a characteristic of the uterine lining that it is very susceptible to hormonal changes. If at any time the hormone level drops too low, the lining shrinks, the circulation is considerably decreased, and the outer damaged part of the lining is cast off. This is always accompanied by a variable amount of bleeding, the process generally taking place over a period of several days. The ensuing menstrual period varies somewhat from one cycle to another, but in general each woman has her own characteristics with respect to it. The flow may vary from light to heavy, it may or may not be preceded by a period of light staining, and it can normally vary in duration from two to seven days.

Menstruation has been defined as "the weeping of a disappointed uterus." This refers to the fact that all of the complicated changes that occur go for naught if a fertilized egg, the result of successful impregnation, fails to come along. Actually an egg is not released in every cycle in every woman. What may appear to be a typical menstrual period coming on at the usual time can result from a cycle of growth in the lining without an egg being formed. Such cycles are termed anovulatory cycles. They are most common in young girls in their early teens and women towards the end of their reproductive lifetime, that is, in their forties. However, they may occur at other times and can alternate with typical ovulatory cycles. When they occur frequently, they may be an important factor in female sterility.

Similarly, menstruation occurs in women taking birth control pills, although here the development of the egg is inhibited and ovulation therefore does not occur. Women who have gone through a menopause and for one reason or another are placed on hormones will also experience a menstrual flow if they stop the hormones for a few days. There is one factor alone which links all these different kinds of menstrual flow: in all cases menstruation occurs when the amount of hormones within the woman's body is suddenly decreased. Once the uterine lining has been built up by

THE FALLOPIAN TUBES

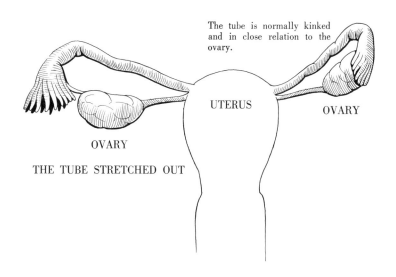

The tube is normally kinked and in close relation to the ovary.

UTERUS

OVARY

OVARY

THE TUBE STRETCHED OUT

SECTION OF THE TUBE AND OVARY

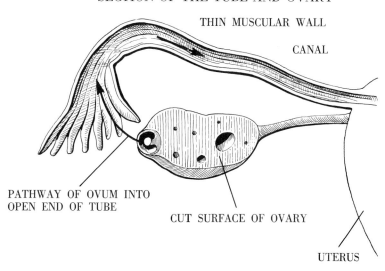

THIN MUSCULAR WALL

CANAL

PATHWAY OF OVUM INTO
OPEN END OF TUBE

CUT SURFACE OF OVARY

UTERUS

FIGURE 12

hormones, it must be sustained by a continued flow of them or it will inevitably collapse and bleed. However, not all bleeding is menstrual in nature. Thus a few women at the time of ovulation may show a small amount of pink discharge due to congestion in the uterine lining at that time. And in some women taking birth control pills, staining or spotting may occur to which the term breakthrough bleeding (BTB) has been applied. BTB may be an indication of inadequate amounts of hormones and is sometimes treated by temporarily increasing the dose of the birth control pill.

The major mass of the uterus is composed of thick bundles of interweaving muscle. These muscles are far thicker than similar muscles used to propel food along in the stomach or intestine. This thick uterine musculature has no value in the nonpregnant state. In fact its contractions, as at the time of menstruation, may lead to colicky pains, the familiar menstrual cramps. The musculature is obviously designed for the purpose of childbirth. During pregnancy, this muscle enlarges enormously in preparation for the eventual labor.

Fallopian Tubes

The fallopian tubes are twin channels which slowly move the egg from the ovary down into the uterus. They are some three inches in length and about the thickness of a lead pencil. The basic structure of the tube resembles that of the uterus: there is an outer layer of muscle and an inner secreting lining. However, here both these layers are far simpler and thinner. (Thus in the rare instances where a fertilized egg implants into the wall of the tube—tubal or ectopic pregnancy—a potentially dangerous state arises, since pregnancy cannot proceed far in this location.) The tube has a trumpet-shaped furrowed expansion at its ovarian end which is in close proximity to the ovary, especially at

EGG DEVELOPMENT IN RELATION
TO THE MENSTRUAL CYCLE

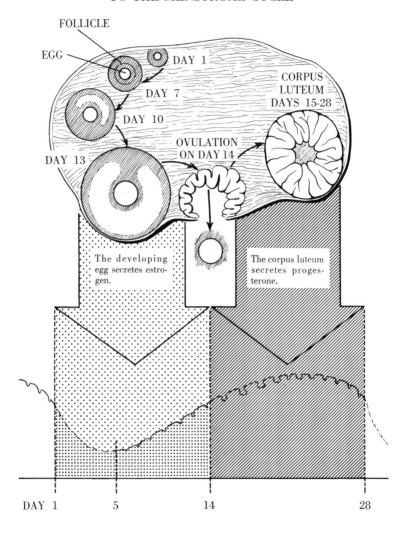

FOLLICLE

EGG

DAY 1

DAY 7

DAY 10

DAY 13

CORPUS
LUTEUM
DAYS 15-28

OVULATION
ON DAY 14

The developing egg secretes estrogen.

The corpus luteum secretes progesterone.

DAY 1   5   14   28

Estrogen produces growth in
the uterine lining. It also causes
the cervix to secrete, the vaginal
lining cells to multiply, and the
breast glands to enlarge.

Progesterone completes the
cycle in the uterine lining in
preparation for pregnancy.

FIGURE 13

the time of ovulation. Then the freshly released egg is gently captured by the tube. If intercourse has occurred during the preceding day or so, sperm may be waiting at this end of the tube. Since the egg can be fertilized only during the first day after its release, conception doubtless often takes place in the outer portion of the tube. It takes the egg some three days to traverse the tube. If the egg is not fertilized, it fragments during this time. Otherwise its cells divide several times during the course of the three-day tubal journey.

Ovaries

The ovaries of a fertile woman are roughly grape-sized, although some variations exist and the two ovaries may not be symmetrical. It is a curious fact that all the egg cells a woman will ever produce are already present in her ovaries at birth. The newborn female infant has hundreds of thousands of tiny immature egg cells scattered about through the ovaries. Less than five hundred of them are destined to enlarge and develop to the point at which they can be released from the ovary and potentially start a new life. (This is based on the simple calculation that a woman's reproductive lifetime is approximately forty years, that she has thirteen menstrual cycles in a year, and generally only one egg matures with each cycle. Forty times thirteen equals 520.)

In contrast with the reckless overabundance and wastefulness that occurs in sperm production, the mature egg cell represents a pampering process. The mature egg cell, which may be referred to as the egg for short, is a strikingly large cell. It is surrounded by a mass of smaller cells which nourish it, the grouping being termed a follicle. In any given menstrual cycle, several follicles may be chosen for growth, but generally only one reaches full maturity. As the follicle enlarges, the egg cell grows bigger and a group of surrounding satellite cells multiply. Soon thereafter a fluid collects within the follicle. A ripe follicle therefore presents a blister-like appearance and gives that part of the ovary a somewhat translucent appearance. The rim of the little blister is composed of cells which secrete increasing amounts of female sex hormones. This secretion, termed an estrogen, produces growth in the lining of the uterus and increasing amounts of a thin secretion of mucus in the cervix. It also causes thickening of the lining cells of the vagina and some enlargement of the little glands of the breasts. Remarkable indeed is the synchronous nature of all these many events in a woman.

The egg is released from the mature follicle most often some 10 to 14 days after the onset of a menstrual period. This shedding of the egg is termed ovulation, perhaps the most basic and important of all reproductive events. The process may be likened to the slow bursting of a skin blister. The egg and its surrounding cells emerge through the opening thus formed. For a brief fateful period the egg may be momentarily free in the abdominal cavity. Indeed, instances are known where an egg shed from one ovary has migrated across the pelvis to enter the tube of the opposite side. The potential hazard of loss of the egg at ovulation is reduced by the behavior of the tube. Its free, congested, and enlarged end expands upward, close to the ovary; thus the newly released egg is almost at once captured and brought within the safe confines of the tube.

Corpus Luteum

If ovulation occurs, pregnancy may be a consequence. But first another sex hormone is necessary properly to prepare the uterus. This hormone is known as progesterone (literally, for gestation or pregnancy). Progesterone quiets down the contractions of the uterus. It also increases the nutrients produced by the uterine lining. It acts on the breasts, stimulating changes that are necessary for the milk production which will occur many months later. It is a trib-

ute to nature's efficiency with leftovers that she assigns
manufacture of this important hormone to the remnants of
the follicle after ovulation. With release of the egg, the
follicle collapses and is temporarily a smaller wrinkled little
structure. Then a new cycle of growth starts up in the lining
cells: they enlarge, accumulate large numbers of tiny fat
droplets, and assume a pale yellow color. For this reason
the new structure has been called the corpus luteum (literally, the yellow body). From the corpus luteum emanates
the progesterone necessary to insure a uterus prepared for
pregnancy and hence the corpus luteum is classified as a
gland of internal secretion. If the newly released egg meets
the sperm and a pregnancy results, the corpus luteum continues to enlarge and secrete for many weeks. Most often,
of course, pregnancy does not result. In the nonpregnant
cycle, the corpus luteum begins to degenerate about two
weeks after ovulation. The amount of hormone it secretes
drops off rather suddenly, most commonly at around the
twenty-eighth day of the cycle.

It is an invariable rule that menstruation will occur
when a woman goes from a higher to a lower sex hormone
level, particularly if the dropoff is abrupt. The drop in secretion from the corpus luteum is indeed an abrupt one. Degenerative changes rapidly occur in the uterine lining, and
discarding of this lining with menstruation inevitably occurs.

Perhaps the menstrual cycle could more accurately be
termed the ovarian cycle. The complicated changes in the
lining of the uterus are completely controlled by the two
hormones secreted by the ovary. The sole exceptions, as we
have noted, are the relatively rare cycles in which ovulation
does not occur, the anovulatory cycles.

The Pituitary

The remarkable cycles that rhythmically occur in the
ovary each month are themselves controlled by a very dis-

PITUITARY REGULATION OF THE OVARY

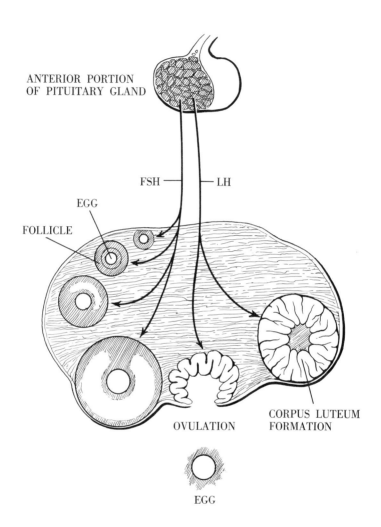

ANTERIOR PORTION
OF PITUITARY GLAND

FSH —— —— LH

EGG

FOLLICLE

OVULATION

CORPUS LUTEUM
FORMATION

EGG

Follicle-stimulating hormone (FSH) controls
follicle growth from day 1 to midcycle. The luteinizing hormone (LH) appears, the egg is released from
the follicle (ovulation) and the corpus luteum forms.

FIGURE 14

tant gland, the pituitary, located at the base of the brain. This is a pea-sized structure in about as inaccessible a location as could be imagined. The pituitary has been called the master gland because its secretions control such other important glands as the adrenals, the pancreas, the ovaries and testes, and even milk formation in the glands of the breasts. As a matter of fact, the growth of all body cells is also attributable to a growth hormone coming from the pituitary. For the ovary, the pituitary has two special chemical messengers. The first stimulates follicles to grow and hence is termed the follicle-stimulating hormone (FSH). When the follicle has reached maturity and the egg is ripe, a second pituitary hormone is responsible for ovulation and the formation of a corpus luteum. It is therefore referred to as the luteinizing hormone (LH). Clearly, FSH and LH are determinant factors in reproduction. Some cases of female sterility are due to failure in the production of these two hormones.

Some of the most remarkable advances in the whole field of reproductive biology in recent years have stemmed from increased understanding and control of the pituitary phase of reproduction. It is now abundantly clear that a woman's reproductive apparatus is a delicately meshed and complicated mechanism. In its simplest essentials, however, the FSH produced by the pituitary in the first part of the cycle leads to growth of the follicle and to estrogen production, with consequent stimulation of the uterus to growth. At the proper time LH appears, ovulation occurs, and the corpus luteum is formed. This leads to further growth and changes in the uterus, insuring a well-prepared nest for the fertilized egg. If pregnancy goes forward, the pituitary cycle is held in abeyance, thus insuring that no further ovulation occurs during pregnancy.

3.
What Makes a Woman Fertile?

THERE IS ONE INESCAPABLE essential needed for fertility in a woman—the maturation of an egg cell. No matter how healthy or potent her mate, all effort will be of no avail unless she produces a fertilizable egg cell. There are women who persistently fail to produce any egg cells whatever, although their menstrual cycles come and go quite regularly. As has already been noted, such cycles are called anovulatory. It has been estimated that perhaps 10 per cent of all menstrual cycles may be anovulatory; they are most common in teenagers and women past forty, but can also occur, interposed with normal cycles, in sexually mature women in their twenties and early thirties. Sometimes an anovulatory cycle can be suspected when the menstrual discharge is markedly different, perhaps a good deal scantier than usual. This is not always the case, however, and it may be altogether impossible to distinguish cycles in which a mature egg has been formed from those without such formation. Sometimes a cycle a bit shorter than usual—say 23 to 24 days instead of 28—perhaps accompanied by less bloating and swelling of the breasts, may be correctly suspected to be a cycle without ovulation. But even then the suspicion may not be well founded, for it may be demonstrated that such a short, somewhat atypical cycle may also have involved egg maturation. In short, cycles without ripening and liberation of an egg may be interposed with many potentially fertile cycles without a woman being aware of it.

A chronic failure to ovulate is the cause of sterility in some women. The number of women with absolute or relative sterility due to failure to form mature eggs is unknown. At one time it was assumed that most barren marriages were due to such failure on the part of the woman. However, all recent investigations indicate that at least half of all sterile marriages are due to difficulties in the male. An inability to form egg cells may be correctable. There are drugs and hormonal agents which can stimulate an ovary to egg formation. Some of these have received considerable newspaper publicity because of an overshoot in the opposite direction: some of the women treated with these agents have had triplets and quadruplets as a result of superovulation. There are of course other reasons for impaired fertility in women, the chief being blockage of the tubes due to old inflammations. The tube may become so obstructed and distorted as a result of infection that the egg and the sperm can never meet. Attempts to correct this by surgical procedures are occasionally successful.

Assuming, however, that a woman does ovulate and that all channels are clear, human reproduction still is relatively inefficient. There is much wastage of eggs and, as we have seen, even more enormous wastage of sperm. It has been calculated that even with couples of known fertility, any single act of intercourse occurring at any time between menstrual periods would result in pregnancy no more often than once in twenty-five to fifty times. This stands in some contrast with the situation found in other forms of life where the female has a definite breeding cycle: with the exception of man and man's close cousins such as the apes, the female will mate only when ripe eggs are present in the ovary, so that any act of mating almost inevitably produces pregnancy. It is possible to increase the fertility of women, however, by applying some of the facts that have been accumulated regarding her reproductive life. With the overwhelming majority of women, making use of such simple facts can raise the possibility of pregnancy, in any given cycle to at least one chance in three. Hence the problem of fertility in most women is simply that of trying to determine when the time of ovulation occurs. Some of the riddles and problems of fertility would immediately vanish were it possible to have a simple, readily recognized sign of ovulation. A knowledge of the time of ovulation would enable a couple to plan their sexual relations so as readily to attain such goals as a desired pregnancy. The converse of this is also true. The rhythm method of birth control is a system devised to diminish or avoid the chance of pregnancy by abstaining from intercourse during the fertile period. Rhythm would be a widely applicable method if the time of ovulation were readily recognizable. There are therefore two fundamental questions to be raised with respect to fertility in women: Is ovulation occurring? When is ovulation occurring? Strictly scientific answers to these questions require tedious and time-consuming efforts on the part of the doctor or his technicians. There are also simpler answers to these questions which we can now consider.

Ovulation is not always an event that is completely hidden and unrecognized. In view of the elaborate changes that go on in a woman during every menstrual cycle, it would be surprising indeed if there were no hints of any sort as to when ovulation is taking place. One of the more dramatic of these is more than a hint—it is a pain experienced in the lower abdomen. The pain may be a sharp stab associated with bloating, or perhaps a dull ache which may last for hours, or merely a sensation of heaviness and congestion which comes on more or less rapidly. It may be felt on both sides of the lower abdomen, nothwithstanding the fact that it originates from the ovary on one side only. Sometimes, when sharp, the pain has been taken for acute appendicitis and operations have been performed. During such an operation a collapsed follicle is to be seen in the ovary, sometimes with a tiny bleeding spot marking the exit point of the egg cell. There can be no question about the existence of ovulation with such an ovarian finding, and the original evidence that it comes in midcycle was derived from such surgical experiences.

Since ovulatory pain typically occurs midway between periods and was first described in the German scientific literature, it came to be known as mittelschmerz (literally, middle pain). Such a midcycle pain occurs in regular fashion in only a few women. With the overwhelming majority, the egg issues from the ovary painlessly. Even in women who experience mittelschmerz there may be cycles in which pain does not occur. When it is present, it may be a most useful fact and worthy of being charted. There are numerous recorded instances of women who have been correctly guided by the midcycle pain to become pregnant, or who conversely have utilized it to avoid pregnancy. Thus one Denver physician reported that his wife successfully planned all her pregnancies in relation to her regularly recurring midcycle pain. By avoiding intercourse prior to and at about the time of the pain, she invariably avoided pregnancy. When another baby was wanted, intercourse at the time of midcycle pain would rather uniformly result in pregnancy.

Unfortunately, since midcycle pain is an uncommon event, we must turn elsewhere for hints on the timing of ovulation. True, once a woman has been told of the events going on within her body, she may observe the previously unnoted changes occurring at this time. Though there may be no outright pain, bloating and lower abdominal distention may be noted. A fair number of women note an increased vaginal discharge of a watery mucus at around the middle of the cycle. Unlike the frequently encountered increase of secretion prior to the menstrual period, the discharge around the middle of the cycle is characteristically more fluid and more abundant. This watery discharge comes from the glands of the cervix, the neck of the womb. It is these glands' response to the increased amount of female hormone that appears prior to the time of ovulation.

It has been shown quite clearly that the change in the secretion occurring somewhat prior to ovulation favors the ascent of sperm. It is also known that sometimes the mucous secretion present in the opening of the cervix is so thick or of such a nature that it may repel or inhibit sperm travel— so-called hostile mucus. When the increased amount of watery secretion occurs within a day or two of the time of midcycle bloating or pain, there can be no doubt about the relationship between the two events. Also noted at this time may be a slight pink staining to the discharge. This results from the congestion of the uterus also brought about by the increased hormone stimulation. As a result, some red blood cells escape from the blood vessels of the lining, often in sufficient numbers to produce a slight pink tinge. This has sometimes been referred to as ovulatory bleeding. Unfortunately, in many women there are irregular variations in the amount of vaginal secretions which are not related to the ovarian cycle. Thus some common vaginal infections, even when mild, may produce enough increased secretion to obliterate other cyclic changes.

There are still other indications which can be used to define the time of ovulation. The lining cells of the vagina go through cyclic changes under the influence of the hormones emanating from the ovary. There is a constant slow shedding of the outermost cells in much the same way as occurs in the skin. These cells can be examined under a microscope and from their appearance a reasonable estimate made as to a woman's hormonal status. In addition to the lining being thin prior to puberty and after the menopause, in the absence of adequate amounts of female hormone the cast-off cells are small, rounder, and transparent. When more hormone is secreted (or taken by mouth) the cells are shed more abundantly, are larger and flatter, and less transparent. These are the cornified cells to which reference was made in the preceding chapter, and indeed they do bear some resemblance to the tough platelike cells of a corn.

Cornified cells are always to be found in the vagina of a healthy woman during her years of reproductive activity. Furthermore, if one examines the shed lining cells at close intervals throughout the cycle, fluctuations in their appearance can be seen. The larger, flatter cornified cells appear in greatest numbers at around the time of ovulation. There is in fact a steady increase in their numbers, reaching a maximum at the time of ovulation. This may readily be seen if one compares a series of smears, starting with one made immediately after the finish of menstruation and continuing through the cycle. However, to make the smears and interpret this series of changes requires that a woman report to the doctor's office fairly frequently. Hence this method of following the cycle is seldom used except in special fertility studies.

A reliable method for determining the time of ovulation is through chemical examination of the urine. After the egg is released, the structure which harbored it is converted into a new gland, the corpus luteum (see Chapter 2). The special hormone this secretes circulates through the body, and some of it in altered form passes out into the urine. Prior to ovulation, the urine fails to contain this substance.

Soon after ovulation has occurred, increasing amounts of this altered hormone can be found. Such urinary assays are time-consuming, expensive, and require daily urine collection. However, they do prove the occurrence of ovulation if this matter is in doubt; they also indicate the day of the cycle on which it has occurred. Of course, this complex method is seldom resorted to except in special circumstances.

The search for a simple indicator of ovulation has led down many byways. For a time it was hoped that electrical changes in the pelvis might prove a useful indicator, but in spite of some favorable initial reports this method has not proved fruitful. More recently, a test was proposed which measured changes in the content of a simple sugar in the secretions coming from the cervix. It was hoped that a characteristic color change on the sensitive paper tape, described as a "fertility tape," would indicate that ovulation was occurring. This too has failed to be a valid test.

There is one kind of data collection that is easy and has been of great value in estimating the time of ovulation. Simple, requiring merely the daily taking of the temperature, it is based on the finding that there are fluctuations in body temperature in women throughout their cycle. In the absence of other circumstances varying from a cold to a gastrointestinal upset, which may alter body temperature, it can be shown that women go through a cycle in which their body temperature moves downward during the first half of the cycle and upward during the second. There are various lines of evidence which indicate that these interesting cycles of body temperature are related to the hormones coming from the ovary. Some of the more pertinent relations between body temperature and hormones have been derived from the following observations:

1. Neither men nor boys show cyclic changes in body temperature. Only small daily variations are seen.

2. Young girls up to the time of puberty are like boys and men in this respect. They exhibit only minor fluctua-

tions in basal body temperature. With the onset of menstruation, an increasing number of cycles may begin to show characteristic temperature changes.

3. In women who have lost their ovaries, the graph of daily body temperature is like that found in boys or men. However, if an estrogen, the hormone of the first phase of the cycle, is administered to such a woman, there may be seen a slow drop in body temperature. If, after this, progesterone, the second hormone of the ovary, is given, a rise in the basal body temperature occurs rather promptly.

4. A fall in basal body temperature, followed by a rise, is precisely the change seen during the normal cycle. The rise produced when the second hormone takes over from the first is known as the *thermal shift*. In the menstrual cycle, the rise in temperature corresponds approximately to the time of ovulation.

Activity of itself causes fluctuations in body temperature. It is therefore necessary to take the temperature in the morning, prior to getting up. The temperature thus recorded is known as the basal body temperature, generally abbreviated to BBT. For convenience and greater ease in reading, a special thermometer known as an ovulation thermometer may be used. The stem of this thermometer records over a smaller range than the usual fever thermometer. It runs from 96 to 100, less than half the range of the standard thermometer. As a result, spacing between degrees is wider and accurate readings are more readily made. Keeping track of the BBT is a standard procedure in most studies of fertility in women. When the findings are clear, it is a simple way of collecting important information. In many women studies of the BBT make it possible to determine that ovulation is taking place, and also the approximate time it occurs during the cycle.

Charting is easily done. A specially lined strip of paper can be used for this purpose (Chart I). On it a woman records the days of her period and the BBT for each day.

The BBT itself is the reading gotten by inserting the thermometer under the tongue (oral temperatures seem to be as accurate for this purpose as rectal ones) each morning prior to arising. The thermometer is maintained under the tongue for a full three minutes and read to the nearest tenth of a degree. The result is entered on the appropriate square of the chart. As this is done for each day of the cycle, a pattern may become apparent. One can see a trend producing a gradual drop in the BBT in the days after the onset of the menstrual period. Perhaps most often around the tenth to fourteenth day, a more or less marked drop will be seen. Then a reversal occurs: the temperature rises within a day or two to a high point which is then steadily maintained until about the time of the next menstrual period. If pregnancy does occur, there is a continued secretion of the temperature-elevating hormone, and a plateau at this elevated level is maintained for months. The midcycle temperature rise followed by a plateau characterizes the thermal shift. A great number of observations indicates that the shift occurs at about the time of ovulation, or shortly thereafter. In the occasionally interposed cycles in which it is known that a woman has not ovulated, the temperature drop, or thermal shift, and the two-week maintenance of the higher temperature all fail to occur.

Of the various methods proposed for keeping track of a woman's reproductive cycle, BBT graphing is by far the most useful. Thus in the graph shown in Chart II you see an average temperature during the menstrual period of approximately 98.5. As can be seen, the temperature tends to drop off so that on the thirteenth day of the cycle the BBT is 97.6. Over the next two days an abrupt rise to 99 is observed, and this is maintained in more or less steady fashion for the next ten days. There can be little doubt that this is a cycle during which ovulation has occurred, with the time of ovulation on about the thirteenth day. Often there may be corroborative data in addition. Thus it may be

OVULATION: BASAL BODY TEMPERATURE

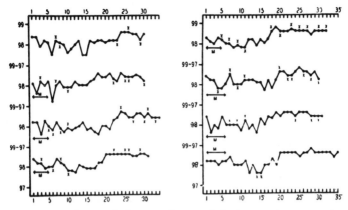

One woman's record showing the use of the temperature curve to avoid conception during seven consecutive months and in the eighth month to start a pregnancy; x = day of exposure to conception. (From Zuck, Ohio State Med. J. 25:1200–1203.)

CHART I

observed that an increased amount of a watery discharge occurred around Days 11 and 12 in such a cycle, and that some bloating or lower abdominal pain was experienced around Day 13 in association with the thermal shift. In short, many of the changes occurring during a cycle of this kind are clearcut and in agreement with one another.

As cycle after cycle is charted, a well-defined pattern may become increasingly evident. In a woman who is regular in her menstrual cycles, the thermal shift is also quite regular, and will occur about midcycle. Hence charting of menstrual cycles and graphing of the BBT can provide especially welcome information in family planning. It can be invaluable in calculating the fertile and infertile periods of a woman's menstrual cycle, thus furnishing the data for the only method of family planning sanctioned by the Roman Catholic Church.

The finding of a well-defined thermal shift in midcycle can be an aid to other contraceptive methods. It is known that the newly released egg can be fertilized for no more than 24 hours. The total duration of the period of fertility

THERMAL SHIFT

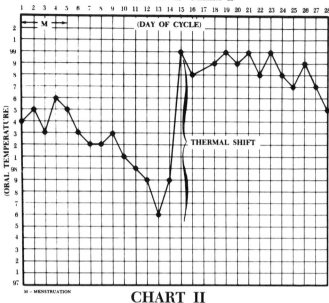

CHART II

in women is thus a limited one. If one were to wait two or three days after the thermal shift has occurred, the likelihood that intercourse would result in a pregnancy would be virtually nil. Utilization of this fact for a series of menstrual cycles is illustrated in Chart I. This represents a series of cycles of a woman who used no contraceptive methods at all. Sexual intercourse is marked out by x's. During the first eight months, intercourse was avoided for several days before and two to three days after the thermal shift. The method was successful as a contraceptive, and pregnancy did not occur. In the ninth month, when pregnancy was desired, intercourse at the time of the thermal shift resulted in a planned pregnancy.

The data furnished by the BBT can be used along with other contraceptive methods to enhance their helpfulness. Thus if, in addition to using the accustomed contraceptive technique, care were taken to avoid intercourse at around the time of ovulation as judged by the temperature graphs, a reduction in the risk of pregnancy would certainly be anticipated.

80

There are drawbacks to the use of the BBT. A cold, a bowel upset, a bladder infection, or any of a number of minor or major illnesses may raise the temperature for a period of time. They will interfere with the establishing of the BBT, perhaps making it impossible to determine a thermal shift. Ovulation may occur, of course, but the associated temperature changes will not be evident. Another by no means infrequent problem is the day-to-day fluctuations in the basal body temperature: there are ups and downs on a random basis which are sometimes hard to interpret. Thus a minor fluctuation down on the tenth day and up on the following day might create a false impression of thermal shift. Sometimes two or three of these up and downswings may occur before a major one followed by a prolonged elevation correctly identifies the time of ovulation. Thus in the charting of some cycles it is possible to identify the time of ovulation only in retrospect.

Often the times of ovulation can be correctly estimated if a record of BBT's is kept over many months. From such a record one could set down the days of ovulation and determine the spread among them. If in a regularly menstruating woman the thermal shift is repeatedly found to occur, say, on Days 12, 13, 14, and 15 and not at other times, reproductive information of the most basic kind can be derived. Such data for a large number of women followed for many years has been accumulated by Dr. Rudolf Vollman, formerly of Switzerland and now with our National Institutes of Health. By also keeping track of intercourse, including isolated instances of intercourse—once in a whole cycle, for example—it has been clearly shown that the time of the most fertile sexual intercourse is approximately two days before the thermal shift. This, as far as we know, means that reasonably fresh sperm are present in the tubes at the time the egg arrives. Conversely, intercourse several days after the thermal shift almost invariably falls into the sterile period.

4.
What Makes a Couple Fertile?

Is it easy or difficult to become pregnant? The answer is: both. Can a healthy young couple select a particular month to initiate pregnancy, and succeed? The answer is they may succeed but they may be overly optimistic. Can a fertile couple pick a preferred season of the year for their baby to born in? The answer is they may succeed but no one will guarantee such a success. The basic facts of human reproduction clearly indicate that the state of pregnancy is not necessarily easy to achieve. This, of course, is not the idea that one gathers from some novels or movies, where a suitable hero meets the heroine and pregnancy results from a single night's rapture. Though this can certainly add to the story interest, the biologist might balk over its improbability. On the day of the chance encounter the heroine would have had to have a ripe follicle in her ovary approaching ovulation. The chances against this are fairly high; besides, intercourse at this time does not necessarily result in conception. Doctor Christopher Tietze has calculated that the chances of a woman becoming pregnant from a single sexual encounter on an unselected day of her reproductive cycle lies somewhere between twenty-five to one and fifty to one. In real life the hero could more easily meet the heroine on any of her many infertile days, say in the last third of the cycle when infertility is absolute.

Again let us repeat: it is not as easy to get pregnant as many people think. Ovulation has to occur. Sperm have to be present in large amounts. Besides, the sperm face a difficult task. Someone has compared the perilous journey they must take to the trials of a swimmer going against the tide for approximately one mile. Even with this herculean task performed, the sperm may just as easily ascend the wrong tube, say the left one when the egg happens to be on the right, and for them it would be a case of love's labors lost. A great many pieces must fall into place before a pattern of pregnancy can be completed. The simple schematic diagrams that show a large egg placidly waiting for one of millions of callers to arrive are deceptively simple. More often there are eggs and there are sperm and never the twain do meet. Human beings have sexual relations because they love and are stirred by one another, and this is a most important distinction between man and the lower animals. In man sex is an act of love. In the animal it is purely reproductive, with the female accepting the male only at the time of ovulation. At other times she is not interested and may even fight him off.

To make an act of love coincide with an act of successful reproduction is one of the tasks of family planning. A healthy couple not using any contraceptive devices can reasonably expect pregnancy to occur within three to six months. However, it may well take up to a year, and most specialists on infertility agree that it is pointless to go through elaborate studies until a year without pregnancy has passed. Sometimes a desired solution to the problem of becoming pregnant is simple. It may be a matter of having sexual relations at the most favorable times of the cycle, and it is always surprising to encounter couples who do not know that there is such a time. Unless one knows about the fertile period of a woman's cycle, much sexual activity will not result in pregnancy. This was pointed out in a famous study done in the early 1930's before knowledge of the fertile period had been worked out and disseminated. This study showed that for fertile couples using no contraceptive methods there were approximately 250 acts of intercourse for every live birth. Left to their own random mating patterns, human beings are relatively sterile when compared to other species.

This situation can be improved considerably because of the expansion of knowledge in this area. The basic principles that one has to know are relatively few. No calculations are necessary, and a simple glance at the calendar should be sufficient. A little cooperation from the male is necessary, of course. The application of a few simple concepts can be expected to result in pregnancy in most couples within a three-month period. Here then is a prescription for getting pregnant and an explanation of some of the underlying facts.

As explained in Chapters 3 and 11, a woman is potentially fertile for only a short span of her entire menstrual cycle. This includes a period of several days before the egg is released from the ovary and extends to no more than 12 to 24 hours after. Most often fertilization of the egg—and pregnancy—comes about when fresh sperm are already lying in wait in the outer part of her tubes. The egg, newly arrived in the tube, must soon encounter sperm or its innate delicacy and fragility will assert itself. What it comes down to is that there are perhaps three days in the cycle in which intercourse could result in pregnancy. The task is to identify these fertile days.

In some women the indicators of oncoming ovulation

are sufficiently well marked so that they can be identified and used in becoming pregnant. One is an increased amount of a watery discharge from the reproductive tract. This is due to the fact that with impending ovulation the increased amount of hormones circulating in the system alter the secretions coming from the cervix. These alterations are such as to favor the entry and movement of sperm. The change in secretion takes place two to three days before ovulation and when it is observed can certainly serve as a useful indicator. Failure to note it does not mean that ovulation is not occurring. Other common factors such as mild infections may conceal its presence.

Shifts in the basal body temperature curve, the BBT (Chapter 3) is a finding most helpful to the planning of pregnancy. Ovulation occurs at the midcycle low point in the temperature curve. Lastly, ovulatory pain, the sharp or dull pain in the lower abdomen which occurs in midcycle, has been shown to be a good indicator of the release of an egg. All of these findings, singly or together, are helpful guidelines to fertile intercourse, not only in any given cycle but also for succeeding ones, for they may tend to group together cycle after cycle.

However, in many women it may be difficult or impossible to identify the time of ovulation by self-observation alone. The change in secretions may not be obvious enough. Certainly many women ovulate with no pain whatsoever. Nor is it always possible to identify the shift in body temperature at the time that it occurs. The drop and the rise may not be sharp, and the time of its occurrence may be clear only in retrospect, when the course of the graph is inspected. Nor is a general knowledge of the extent of the fertile period enough. Women who have been using the rhythm method of birth control will of course know approximately when their fertile period is. By the usual method of calculation, however, much of this period of seven to ten days is well after the time of the actual ovulation. Take the case of a woman with regular 28-day cycles in whom the fertile period is calculated to begin on Day 9 and extend through Day 18. In a cycle in which she ovulates on Day 11, she becomes infertile on Day 12 so that the last six days of the "fertile period" are actually infertile. Intercourse on Days 13 or 14 of such a cycle, which would generally be regarded as occurring during a time of great fertility, would *not,* in fact, result in pregnancy.

There is a simple rule of thumb based upon many observations which can be helpful in pregnancy planning. It has been derived from studies of isolated acts of intercourse and of artificial insemination done perhaps only once in a given cycle. It pinpoints the day on which intercourse is most likely to result in pregnancy. It presupposes a reasonable amount of regularity in the menstrual cycles but does take into account the fact that some women have short, others longer cycles. The method is simplicity itself:

1. Average up the last three cycle lengths.
2. Divide this average by 2 and subtract 2 days from it. This gives the day on which a single act of intercourse is most likely to result in pregnancy.

As an example, a woman whose last three menstrual cycles have been 27, 29, and 28 days has an average cycle length of 28. Dividing this by 2 yields Day 14; subtracting 2 from this yields Day 12. It would be reasonable to expect that intercourse on Day 12 of her cycle might result in pregnancy. As another example, in a woman whose cycles were 25, 23, and 24 days, average cycle length would be 24 days. Half this is 12, and therefore the best day for fertile intercourse would be Day 10 of the cycle. For the few women whose cycles are on the longer side, a similar calculation can be made with a further alternative. The alternative is to subtract 16 days from the average length of the cycle. Thus in a woman whose menstrual cycles average out to 34 days, the first rule of thumb gives us Day 15, as the best day (one half of 34 less 2). The alternative method gives us Day 18 (34 less 16). It would doubtless be best to have relations on both these days. With longer and more variable cycles, simple calculations of this kind cannot be relied on, and in fact a physician's advice should be asked.

The chances of becoming pregnant are, of course, further increased if intercourse is repeated on several days at around the calculated day of maximum fertility. Thus if the day of maximum fertility is Day 12, the chances of pregnancy would certainly be increased by intercourse on either or both of Days 11 and 13 also. With many young healthy males such frequency of intercourse does not diminish the sperm count. However, too frequent intercourse can lower the number of sperm furnished at any particular ejaculation.

What advice can we give to the male as eager to share the joys of paternity as his wife is to experience the glories of maternity? Clearly, it would be for him to utilize his sperm resources maximally at around the time of his wife's fertile days. One way to do this is to refrain from having intercourse too soon and too frequently after the menstrual period ends. Some couples who are anxious to become parents have patterns of sexual activity which are partially determined by the menstrual period and which may be unfavorable for reproduction. After a period of abstinence imposed by the menstrual flow of, say, five, six, or sometimes seven days, they may have intercourse several times in the ensuing days. They then experience a letup in sexual interest or activity at what would correspond to the time of maximum fertility.

For reproductive purposes it would be better to prolong the period of abstinence until close to the day of maximum fertility. Intercourse repeated at around this time would assure the highest possible sperm counts and thus favor fertility. It is perhaps of interest in this connection that for thousands of years orthodox Jews have obeyed the precept of not having sexual relations until seven days after the menstrual flow has ceased. In the average woman this would bring her to Days 12 or 13, which of course are the days of maximum fertility. The reason for the injunction thus practiced by this wise and ancient group is shrouded in the mysteries of time, but its biologic basis is certainly a well-grounded one.

The most favorable number of times for the male to have sexual relations at the time of fertility is not known and may vary from man to man. Some men can have intercourse daily for several days at a time without an unfavorable lowering of the sperm count. This is particularly likely to be true if a period of abstinence after the close of the menstrual period has been observed. It has been well established that the presence of a large amount of sperm is favorable to fertility. The excess numbers, though they cannot take part in fertilization, somehow favor the chances that a single sperm will be successful. For this reason some authorities have advocated that intercourse be repeated within a few hours, if possible, on the day of greatest fertility. Intercourse within a few hours will furnish at least 25 per cent more sperm than were present initially and might thereby increase the possibility of fertilization.

Still a further aid in increasing the number of sperm available is the woman's positioning after intercourse. Couples anxious for pregnancy should not waste semen. Much semen is wasted because of avoidable spillage. Thus some of it often leaks out when the husband withdraws—more perhaps in certain positions than in others. This occurs even when the couple has intercourse in the usual position, with the woman supine and extended. Such wasting of semen is greatly reduced by this simple precaution: the woman should bring her thighs up towards her abdomen *before* the husband's withdrawal. When fully brought up, her heels will be off the bed, a position which can be more easily maintained if she supports her knees with her arms or if one or two pillows are placed under the heels. The thighs should be kept in this elevated position for twenty minutes or more after intercourse. This position pools the semen at a level lower than the vaginal opening and, since it also increases its holding capacity, leakage is avoided. With the same end in mind, the wife should not get up too soon and should avoid laughing, coughing, sneezing, or other acts which may tend to raise the pressure within the abdomen and force semen out. In a woman whose anatomy is normal, lying flat on the back with the legs drawn up tends to keep the cervix, into which the sperm must ascend, either dipped into or otherwise in closer relation to the main mass of the semen. There are some women whose uteruses are tipped into abnormal positions. Thus in the condition known as retroversion, the uterus may be in a position opposite of normal, and the cervix can point forward instead of backward. To increase the chances of such women getting pregnant, lying on the side or even on the abdomen may be advised by the doctor.

When attention is paid to such simple measures as selecting the most fertile day and following the correct positioning after intercourse, previous difficulties in achieving pregnancy can be overcome. Observations show that intercourse several times at around the fertile day will, in the average couple, raise the chances of becoming pregnant to about one in three in a given cycle. It is to be remembered that even with good data for calculating the time of ovulation, and with the best efforts of the willing couple, pregnancy is not likely to result from any of the sexual efforts in a single cycle. Even when very delicate tests to indicate the time of ovulation are performed, such as daily checking of the urine for hormones, the best that has been reported is approximately a fifty-fifty chance of pregnancy for that cycle.

In short, a couple should not expect to hit the pregnancy target with their first try in the first month. Rather, as the old saying has it, if at first you don't succeed, try, try again.

Also the goal should be attempted in a relaxed, not a desperate manner. There is no experience between human beings which should have more mutuality of effort and positiveness of feeling than that which goes into efforts to achieve parenthood.

When Infertility Is a Problem

It has been shown that approximately 10 per cent of married couples in the United States are involuntarily infertile. This revelation can come as a great shock to couples who have used contraceptives perhaps for years only to face a failure to conceive as the months go by without contraception. It should be borne in mind that reduced fertility becomes more of a problem with the passage of years. Everything else being equal, pregnancy is more likely for a couple in their twenties than in their thirties, and becomes increasingly remote for a couple in their forties. If they truly desire to become parents, couples should not keep postponing parenthood year after year. However, one need not push the panic button if after some months of intercourse without contraception the desired pregnancy has not occurred. One need not conclude that a fertility problem exists short of a year or so of active trying. But the possibility that one is dealing with diminished fertility does increase with the passage of the months, especially if pregnancy does not result after following some of the advice mentioned above. What should be done then?

By far the simplest and most logical first step is to examine the man. Contrary to many people's notions, study has revealed that an unexpectedly high incidence of sterility originates with the man. It has been estimated that at least 30 per cent of barren marriages are due to the male. For this reason, and because of the greater ease of making the appropriate examination, an infertility study should start with an examination of the husband's semen.

What Makes a Couple Fertile?

The semen is examined soon after ejaculation: the amount is measured, a sperm count performed and an attempt is made to grade the motility of sperm cells. At one time it was thought that counts below 50 million sperm per cc (a cc is about one-quarter of a teaspoon) would result in infertility. It has been shown, however, that many males with counts considerably lower than this can achieve fatherhood, especially if the low count is not associated with other abnormalities. In some cases no sperm are found at all, a condition termed azoospermia. This is generally due to some congenital disorder, to inflammation, or some other kind of damage which has attacked both testicles or their ducts. Thus, if inflammation has blocked off both spermatic ducts, sexual drive and performance may be adequate, but, a semen specimen will be delivered composed of prostatic and seminal vesicle fluids only, and completely lacking in sperm. This condition. if irreversible, means of course that fatherhood is impossible.

A variety of subnormal findings are more frequent than a complete absence of sperm. The following are some of the findings likely to be associated with a reduction or absence of fertility on the part of the male:

1. A semen volume of less than 2 cc (less than half a teaspoon).
2. A sperm count of less than 20 million per cc.
3. Actively motile sperm cells less than 40 per cent of the total.
4. Sluggish sperm with motility ratings of under 2+ on a scale of 0 to 4+.

There often are combinations of these findings, such as a small total number of sperm with poor motility or exhibiting many abnormalities of shape or size. The greater the number of abnormalities found together, the greater the degree of infertility is likely to be.

There are other rarer causes which may impair the male's fertility. Normal semen usually clots soon after the ejaculation and then tends to liquefy in the ensuing fifteen minutes. Instances have been observed where this clotting-liquefying mechanism goes awry. Sometimes the semen deposited in the vagina forms a solid tight white clump which tends to fall out like a little ball and never undergoes proper liquefaction.

There are steps that can be taken to improve one or another aspect of the male's contribution. Where intercourse is too frequent, cutting down on its frequency can produce a desirable elevation of the sperm count. But intercourse which is too infrequent is also a problem. Random intercourse, perhaps only once a week, lowers the probability of pregnancy too much. Some authorities feel that a rather common condition of the veins known as a varicocele may have deleterious effects on sperm formation. (A varicocele is a distention of the veins surrounding a spermatic cord.) As explained in Chapter 2, sperm formation goes on best several degrees below body temperature. It has been argued that tight shorts which bring the testicles up close to the body throughout the day may have an adverse influence on sperm formation in some men. (It is clear that no generalizations can be made, for in one survey of fertile couples one-third of the males were noted to be wearing this type of shorts.)

The enlarged veins of a varicocele are thought to raise the temperature within the scrotum and could be a contributing factor in some cases of male infertility. Some experts claim that they can recognize the effect of higher-than-normal temperatures by counts which are normal but with sluggish or otherwise abnormal sperm. The fact is that cases have been reported where simple operative procedures on a varicocele have promptly improved the findings in the semen and pregnancy has resulted. Obviously, such a procedure would be performed only where the other possibilities that might interfere with fertility had been looked into.

In 70 per cent of infertility analyses, the difficulty is

with the woman. A great many conditions may impair a woman's capacity to ovulate. Certainly some sterile women fail to ovulate month after month, however regular or irregular their menstruation may be. Marked degrees of obesity may be associated with such a kind of infertility. So also may disorders of the thyroid or adrenal glands or other glandular abnormalities. In a few women failure to ovulate arises because of a defect in the master gland, the pituitary. Until recently, this form of infertility was very likely to be permanent. However, it is now possible to give agents which either increase the output of the pituitary or stimulate the ovary directly, and ovulation results. Indeed, in some instances superovulation occurs and previously sterile women have been delivered of twins, triplets, and even quadruplets as a result of the treatments. The best way of correcting the faulty pituitary-ovary relationship in such women is still under active study.

Anatomical malformations may be responsible. A large polyp of the cervix or multiple fibroid tumors of the uterus may occasionally alter or distort the canal and interfere with the mechanisms involved in becoming pregnant. Perhaps the most common cause for female infertility is a blockage of the fallopian tubes. Such a block most often results from a previous inflammation. When inflammation of the tube heals, the delicate folded lining can become so distorted, scarred, or adherent that blockage results. The existence of a block is determined by a tubal patency test, known as the Rubin test. In this procedure a gas or iodized oil is injected under some pressure into the uterine cavity. If the tubes are open, the injected material runs up through them and the entire pathway may be visualized by X ray. Some kinds of tubal blockage can be corrected by a surgical procedure. Also in some instances forcing air through the tube when doing the Rubin test may seemingly blow it open or unblock it.

In some women it may be shown that even though ovulation is occurring, the tubes are open, and there is no anatomical abnormality, infertility may nevertheless exist. It may then be due to an infection within the vagina or the cervix inimical to the sperm. There are factors present in some women that may severely impair the performance of sperm. For instance, the mucus found in the cervical canal may be tough and hard to penetrate. Or as a result of infection or other conditions it may contain substances which attack or immobilize sperm—the so-called "hostile mucus." Studies of the sperm deposited in women's vaginas also indicate that great variations in their length of life exists; in a few women vaginal factors which are quite lethal to sperm have been noted.

Even with the most detailed investigations, no specific reason for failure to conceive may be uncovered. It has been postulated that emotional factors may play a role. These are difficult to identify with any degree of certainty. Perhaps in some tense and nervous women an emotional state can, through some physical mechanism, interfere with the possibility of pregnancy. It is difficult to be sure what this mechanism might be or whether in fact it really exists. Some women get no pleasure out of sex, experience no orgasm, may be very negative or frigid about the sexual relationship, yet conceive with ease, their psychological attitudes in no way hampering their fertility.

That an apparent sterility can undergo sudden reversibility has been shown by some couples after the adoption of a baby. The wife then becomes pregnant, sometimes a short time after the adoption. The meaning of this phenomenon has been argued back and forth. Its existence indicates plainly that unexpected pregnancy can result even in couples with a history of many years of sterility who are driven to adoption in order to have the joys of family living. All experience in the area of sexual reproduction indicates that it is a mistake always to judge future achievement by past performance.

The Reduction of Fertility: BIRTH CONTROL

5.
Barriers:
Condom,
Diaphragm, Cap

$\mathbf{T}$HE CONDOM IS A thin latex rubber covering for the penis which is worn during intercourse. As a contraceptive device the condom, in one form or another, has been available for centuries. London handbills several hundred years old, extolling the values of a woven linen sheath, inform us of the modern condom's forerunners. Later, fish bladders began to be used. But the mass-production phase of this device was made possible only with the vulcanization of rubber a century or so ago.

It has been authoritatively estimated that more than half a billion condoms are manufactured each year in the United States, of which only an insignificant part is exported. The total world production probably exceeds one billion per year, thus making the condom the most widely used and also one of the most effective contraceptive methods known. The widespread popularity of this device is readily accounted for. When rolled up, it is small and inconspicuous. It is therefore easily carried about, and it is cheap and readily disposable. It can be donned by the male in a matter of a few seconds. Since the semen is collected at the tip end, proof of effectiveness as a contraceptive is immediately available.

The condom manufacturing process is virtually completely automated. Automated testing procedures are incorporated into the production line which automatically discard condoms with thin spots or blisters or pinhole defects. The products of the better manufacturers may be relied on without further testing. Since 1938, condoms have been subject to inspection by Federal authorities and notable improvements in the quality of the resulting product has occurred. However, there is still some variability in the output from different manufacturers. Condoms under various trade names are sold in most drugstores. It is probably wiser to purchase these items from a drugstore than from other less reliable outlets.

The latex rubber condom is a thin, almost transparent cylinder some seven inches in length and roughly corresponding to the dimensions of the erect penis. As with a balloon, its open end has a slight thickening and thus forms an encircling ring. Some condoms have a small nipple-like reservoir at the closed end for semen collection.

About the only manipulative procedure one might have to be shown with the condom is how to roll it up if an unrolled one is purchased. This is readily done by inserting two fingers into it and rolling the thickened base evenly up over the fingers. The condom has to be in the rolled-up state for use. It is readily applied by reversing the above procedure: the rolled-up condom is applied over the head of the penis and unrolled down its length. With a normal erection, there is a reasonably firm pressure exerted by the remaining unrolled portion of the condom at the base of the penis. This snugness of fit to the shaft helps keep the condom in place.

Use of the condom is simplicity itself and there are few precautions that need be observed. It is generally advised that the condom be put on in such a manner as to leave a small space at the tip end to collect the ejaculate. Soon after the orgasm, the erect penis becomes smaller and flaccid. It may therefore shrink away from the condom in such a manner that, upon withdrawal, the condom may be left behind in the vagina. This need not necessarily present any difficulty but is best avoided, since some spillage of semen may occur over the vulvar region. It can be avoided by having the man hold the base of the condom around the penis as he withdraws.

It is quite rare for a condom to slip off the penis during intercourse, and equally unusual for it to break during the act. In either of these two untoward situations, prompt use of a vaginal foam contraceptive would probably be the most effective means of coping with the risk of pregnancy. If none is available, a prompt douche would be of some value.

If this were to occur during the safe part of the cycle— say the week before menstruation—one would have little reason to fear the possibility of pregnancy. The fact of the matter is that when used with care the condom is one of the more effective contraceptive methods. It at least equals the equivalent feminine barrier, the diaphragm, in contraceptive effectiveness, and has been successfully used by many couples throughout the years of their married life. One test of a contraceptive is its acceptability year in, year out. In this respect also the condom ranks high. Couples who have accepted it may feel little reason for shifting to another method.

But despite the many good things that can be said for it, the condom has had a singular lack of acceptance in certain quarters. It is not one of the techniques stressed at planned parenthood centers, which traditionally have offered methods giving control of conception to the woman—such as the diaphragm. Perhaps also the condom suffers from lack of prestige, a factor not to be underestimated. It is well known that consumers often will buy a large, complicated item when a smaller, less complex, and more easily handled one can serve them just as well. (The more imposing item seems to create more confidence.) From this viewpoint the condom is a humble little item indeed. It is often sold in men's toilets and at gasoline stations, and even in drugstores it constitutes one of the so-called "whisper items." In many areas it is sold not as a contraceptive item which is, of course, its major use, but rather as an accessory "for the prevention of disease." This, too, manages to give it unworthy associations. Lastly, the condom has been associated with illicit, premarital, or extramarital sexual intercourse. When found in a man's possession it may give him the reputation of being a Casanova. Indeed Casanova, one of the great lovers in history—by his own confession at least —recommended the condom highly, referring to it as "the English riding cap."

The condom has survived all of these associations because it is in fact a sensible and useful item. It may be recommended by a doctor in a variety of circumstances. It may be physically and psychologically easier to use on a honeymoon, where the bride is likely to have other problems without getting involved with diaphragms or other devices. With a woman for whom the pills are forbidden for one or another medical reason and who is unable to use the diaphragm, the condom may be one of the most effective of the remaining available methods. Also after childbirth, before the woman's reproductive tract has returned to its previous dimensions, the condom may be of value. At this stage, the old diaphragm may not fit and the pill may not be used if the mother wants to nurse her child. Lastly, the condom may be of value in combination with other techniques. Thus, a couple relying primarily on the foam or cream method might enhance the protection by utilizing the condom at around the time of maximum fertility.

Barriers: Condom, Diaphragm, Cap

There are, however, two criticisms that have been made of the condom—one physical, the other psychological. On the physical side, the condom does act to diminish sensation. This complaint is much more likely to be heard from the man than from the woman. Madame de Sévigné in the famous letters to her daughter wrote that it was "an armor to pleasure, and a cobweb to safety." Neither of these statements is correct. Furthermore, the dulling of sensation produced by the condom is not always unwelcome, since it enables many men pleasurably to prolong the act of intercourse. In addition a well controlled and motivated man can initiate intercourse without use of the condom, donning it later in the act. This has been criticized on the grounds that a small amount of secretion containing sperm may leak out unnoticed during sexual excitement (which probably does occur, but quite rarely). Everything we know about the sterility associated with low sperm counts makes it seem most unlikely that unnoted leakage of this kind could raise the hazards of pregnancy. Of course, contraceptive manuals which are rigidly committed to showing how to gain maximum protection from whatever method is used might not endorse the use of the condom except from the beginning of the sexual act.

The psychological and perhaps esthetic objection that the condom acts as a barrier to complete physical intimacy between a man and a woman may be a reason for rejection by a particular couple. Some have felt that the closeness of the most intimate of all human relations should not be blunted in any respect. They therefore further argue that it is desirable for the man to have a vaginal ejaculation. When the condom is used, its barrier action on the semen makes it appear to be a hazard or a danger. It has been said that the wife may come to regard the husband's semen as something unwelcome, thus creating in her an attitude which is negative and undesirable. To what extent feelings of this kind actually prevail is not known. If they do exist, they are doubtless far outweighed by the negative feelings toward an unwanted pregnancy.

The Diaphragm

The diaphragm was invented in 1882 by a German physician, Mensinga, and his version of this device is still in use. The diaphragm is a dome of rubber enclosing a round or oval flexible spring. A contraceptive jelly or cream is placed within the dome of the diaphragm, and applied also to the diaphragm's rim. The use of such a jelly is an important addition to the diaphragm's effectiveness and *should not be omitted*. To facilitate insertion into the vagina, the diaphragm is compressed and pushed in and up; either the fingers or a special inserter can be used for this. The diaphragm fits snugly against the vaginal wall, behind and to either side of the cervix. In front it is held in position by the pressure it exerts against the vaginal wall and the back of the pubic bones. When correctly positioned, the cervix is completely covered.

To stay thus in position, the diaphragm must come in the correct size. This requires a fitting by the physician, who measures the patient's vagina by inserting one of a series of rings of graduated size. He selects the one which produces a snug fit, and writes a prescription for a diaphragm of corresponding size, most often about 75 to 85 millimeters—about 3 inches. The necessity for such a fitting —and also for a larger diaphragm after the birth of the first baby—is one of the few practical drawbacks to the widespread use of the diaphragm. In addition, the woman must be instructed in the techniques for inserting and removing the device. Though this ordinarily presents no difficulty, some women—especially if they are obese, have short fingers, or have a mental block against inserting objects vaginally—may have trouble with the use of the diaphragm.

There are women who wear the diaphragm for several

THE DIAPHRAGM AND CONTRACEPTION

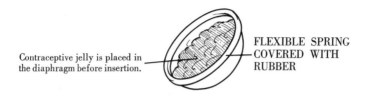

Contraceptive jelly is placed in the diaphragm before insertion.

FLEXIBLE SPRING COVERED WITH RUBBER

SECTION OF THE FEMALE PELVIS
WITH THE DIAPHRAGM IN POSITION

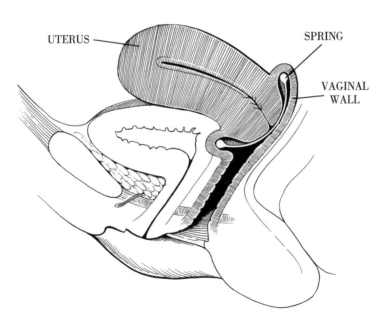

UTERUS

SPRING

VAGINAL WALL

The diaphragm is held in position by outward pressure against the vaginal walls.

FIGURE 15

days on end, but this is not desirable: it should be washed in soap and water and dusted with cornstarch (not talcum) between uses. Some birth control authorities advise patients to have two diaphragms, using them alternately, as one does with toothbrushes. In any event the diaphragm must be removed for the menstrual flow.

Once the technique of insertion and removal has been mastered, the diaphragm provides an excellent, well-established method of contraception. Some women prefer to insert it nightly in routine fashion, others do so only when intercourse is anticipated. The position of the diaphragm is checked with each insertion. In order to do this properly, a woman must learn to recognize the feel of her own cervix, which has a firm, unyielding quality in contrast to the vaginal walls which give way with pressure. In terms of familiar tissues, the vaginal wall feels like the cheek, the cervix like the tip of the nose. Firm pelvic tissues plus snugness of fit are necessary for the diaphragm to work. With the diaphragm correctly fitted, the finger cannot work its way over and around the front end. If it can, as might be the case when a woman resumes using her old diaphragm after the birth of her baby, then a dislodgment of the diaphragm during intercourse is possible. In some women the stretching or changes produced by repeated childbirths may make it difficult to secure proper fit with the usual diaphragm. There are some modifications of the usual models which may then be useful. Occasionally, in particular cases, the diaphragm method cannot be applied at all because of laxness of supporting tissues.

In theory, a fitted diaphragm alone should form an impenetrable barrier to the cervix. In actual practice, the special contraceptive jellies especially made for use with the diaphragm materially add to the reliability of this method. Approximately half a teaspoon of contraceptive jelly is placed within the dome of the diaphragm—the part which is to be up against the opening of the cervix—and a small amount of the jelly is also rubbed around the rim. This not only acts as a seal, increasing adherence of the rubber to the tissues, but also takes care of any stray sperm that might conceivably have worked their way around to the edge of the rubber barrier.

Diaphragms are made of fairly heavy rubber, considerably thicker than that found in the condom. Like all rubber, it may be subject to deterioration with the passage of the years, a process which is accelerated by heat and exposure to air. Accordingly, a diaphragm is best changed every couple of years. If nothing has happened during this period to change a woman's internal measurements, then a replacement of similar size is all that needs to be requested. But if there have been marked changes in body weight, or a pregnancy, or possibly a pelvic operative procedure, then a refitting may be necessary.

For many decades, the diaphragm was entrenched as the standard contraceptive method. It was the one most frequently demonstrated and made available to women attending birth control clinics. Innumerable married women and brides-to-be consulted their gynecologists for fitting and instruction in the diaphragm. One reason for its favor was said to be the great virtue of placing the control of pregnancy in a woman's hands (women being regarded as more reliable, men less so in this respect). To use it properly, of course, a woman had to be well instructed, well fitted, and well motivated. Once these requirements were met, the diaphragm and jelly method remained the most effective of the widely used contraceptive techniques until the advent of the pill. Indeed, some doctors who still have reservations about the pill advocate the diaphragm as involving less tampering with bodily organs. With a younger generation of wives increasingly turning to the pill, the diaphragm still continues to have widespread usage. Where the pill cannot be used, the diaphragm is most likely to be the next recommended method.

Cervical Cap

The cervical cap is a contraceptive device designed to fit snugly over the cervix. Originally made of metal, ivory, or rubber, the more recent models are of clear lucite. Models come in three different sizes ranging from one to one and one-half inches. They have a tapering, dome-shaped appearance arranged so that some degree of adherence to the cervix is assured. When fitted, the cap lies snugly against the cervix but does not compress it; a small space is left between the interior of the plastic dome and the opening of the canal of the cervix. It is generally recommended that some contraceptive jelly or cream be placed in the dome of the cap just as with the diaphragm. However, this does not seem to be necessary to its effectiveness as a contraceptive. Cervical caps may be fitted to some women who cannot wear the diaphragm for anatomical reasons. On the other hand, in women who have a short cervix or a distorted one following childbirth, or the common condition known as a cervical erosion—a kind of inflammation—the cap cannot or should not be used.

The cap is far more widely used in Europe than in the United States and, in fact, is far more popular there than is the diaphragm. Its contraceptive effectiveness is equal to that of the diaphragm. Among the advantages that have been claimed for it are that it can be left in place for days, or even from one menstrual period to the next. The construction of the cap is such that even if a menstrual flow unexpectedly starts, the flow can work its way out around the cap. A well-fitted cervical cap is less likely to be dislodged by intercourse than the diaphragm. The importance of this has been pointed up by recent studies, which indicate that one of the reasons for failure of the diaphragm is dislodgment during active intercourse. However, the technique of inserting and removing the cap is more difficult to learn than the equivalent procedure for the diaphragm. A certain amount of deftness is required on the part of the

THE CERVICAL CAP AND CONTRACEPTION

Contraceptive jelly is placed in the cap before insertion.

RIGID PLASTIC OR SIMILAR MATERIALS

SECTION OF THE FEMALE PELVIS
WITH CERVICAL CAP IN POSITION

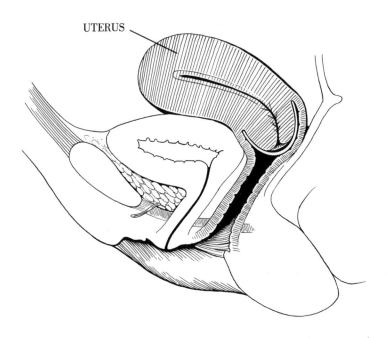

UTERUS

FIGURE 16

woman and in some instances, for those who cannot learn the technique, monthly visits to the doctor's office are necessary. A major drawback to more widespread use of the cap has been the admitted problem of teaching the woman to insert and remove the device. In a few instances a reasonable alternative may be to instruct the husband in the placement or removal of it.

The fact that the cap can be worn for long periods at a time, thereby divorcing its insertion or removal from the sex act itself, is of course an advantage. Only rarely does the accumulation of odorous discharge require that the cap be removed frequently for cleansing purposes. The lucite cap may become somewhat discolored with the passage of time, but otherwise is good for several years of use without change. The anatomical changes that may occur as a result of pregnancy may require a larger-sized cap after the birth of the baby. The cervical cap seems to be an underutilized birth control technique in the United States, one to which more attention should be paid. However, it is not likely to achieve more widespread popularity in the foreseeable future. This is due to the advent of intrauterine contraceptive devices with their special advantages of not needing removal and insertion for the menstrual periods, and because of the widespread acceptance of the pill.

It is an interesting statistical fact that all three of the barrier methods—condom, diaphragm, cap—turn out to have about the same degree of effectiveness as birth control methods, and that is quite considerable. Collectively they rank just below the pill in year-in and year-out reliability. From this viewpoint there is no significant difference between them—nothing to make one choose the male method, the condom, as against the female method, the cap or diaphragm. Other factors, however, may have to be considered with respect to choice (see Chapter 10).

6.
Foams, Creams, and Jellies

As we have seen, the diaphragm plus a contraceptive jelly especially designed for it has been the standard contraceptive method taught and widely practiced in the United States for some decades. The method is somewhat cumbersome, requiring some dexterity for insertion, plus some knowledge of anatomy. With some couples, the diaphragm may need to be inserted every night. If it is not in place when lovemaking starts, then the lovemaking may have to be interrupted. Some ardent couples unwilling to slow down occasionally "take the chance"— and occasionally their passion is rewarded with an unplanned pregnancy. Thus the difference between effectiveness in theory and effectiveness in practice may be considerably greater than the physician at a birth control clinic would anticipate. Emotional blocking over the need for handling the genitals on the part of the woman or a "taking the chance just this once" attitude are not the only reasons for incomplete effectiveness of this otherwise standard method. As noted in Chapter 5, relaxation of supporting structures following the birth of one or more babies, when combined with variations in sexual positioning plus perhaps unusually forceful movements in intercourse, can occasionally contribute to diaphragm dislodgement. In short, even the widely used time-honored diaphragm method has its notable drawbacks. Since neither patients nor doctors have been satisfied with the standard diaphragm-plus-jelly technique, there has always been an interest in simplification, particularly in the search for a method which would bypass the need for the diaphragm. The search soon turned to the area of creams and jellies to be used without the diaphragm.

To be fully effective and therefore acceptable, a contraceptive agent of this type would require easy administration and good dispersal within the vagina. In addition, it should contain an ingredient of high sperm-killing efficacy which at the same time would be nonirritating both to the vaginal tissue and of course to the male. Lastly, the use of an agent which could act as a barrier (much as the rubber of the diaphragm acts as a barrier) would also contribute to contraceptive effectiveness simply by blocking the passageway into the uterus, thus preventing ascent of the sperm. To this end there have appeared a number of creams, foams, and jellies. These are dispensed in different ways and are by no means equal in effectiveness. Actual experience has shown that some can be used with reasonable reliability; others, however, have a contraceptive efficiency lower than is acceptable to many couples involved in family planning.

Any method which is only moderately effective may be of use to some couples who are attracted merely by its simplicity. But in that case they must be willing to accept a pregnancy if it occurs despite the taking of some precautions. The methods to be described in this chapter are in fact less effective than the preceding ones. However, if combined with an additional method, such as the condom, some of them would form very effective combinations and should be weighed with this in mind.

Sperm, like all free cells, are fairly delicate; there are many substances which are harmful to them. This is true even of plain tap water, so that just douching after intercourse will destroy many sperm. Though douching is not reliable and is not a recommended birth control method, it can serve in a pinch when nothing else is available. Acid substances, such as vinegar and lemon juice, even when well diluted with water, can kill off sperm at a concentration which is not harmful to the vaginal tissues. Most of the foams, suppositories, and similar contraceptive agents rely upon one or another well-established chemical agent with a high sperm-killing ability. The most common of these agents is a chemically modified alcohol known as nonyl-phenoxy-poly-ethoxy-ethanol. Even when considerably diluted, this agent will immobilize sperm on contact in forty seconds or less.

Foams. The foams have had a high level of patient acceptability, more so than some of the related products. They are supplied with a measuring device, distribute well, and form a mass of tiny bubbles which according to direct observations acts as a barrier. Their sperm-killing potency is high and their contraceptive record quite good. It has been recommended that a double dose be used to increase effectiveness.

The principles behind foam formation are in every respect similar to those of the lathering shaving creams and similar products dispensed in aerosol cans. Several important precautions are worthy of note:

1) Foam should be used within one hour before having intercourse. If more than an hour has passed, a second dose should be administered. As was already mentioned, some experts recommend a double dose each time, especially for women who have had one or more babies.

2) As with many other products designed to be used

intravaginally, there should be no douching for at least six to eight hours afterwards. In fact, it is not necessary to douche when the foams are used. With the passage of time the minute bubbles comprising the foam collapse, and relatively little residue is left.

Tablets. A variant on the aerosol foam has been a tablet to be placed high in the vagina, which on contact with moisture produces a bubbly, sperm-killing froth. The rate at which the tablet disintegrates and releases foam is dependent in considerable measure on the amount of moisture available. If relatively little moisture is present in the vagina, a slower-than-anticipated rate of foaming may occur. Hence it is generally recommended that the tablet be moistened with water or saliva before insertion, and that upwards of fifteen minutes be allowed for it to act. It is probable that as sexual stimulation proceeds, protection from the tablet may increase. In addition, further moisture will be provided with the ejaculation of semen. However, direct observation indicates that there may not be a uniform dispersal of foam in some users. Also, some women have complained of a burning or other mild local irritative reaction as the tablet disintegrates. Occasional similar complaints have been heard from husbands also. Hence, despite simplicity, the foam tablet is inferior to the preparations delivering an aerosol foam. Also, in contrast to the foam which acts at once, at least fifteen minutes must elapse for proper disintegration of the tablet.

Creams. There are several contraceptive creams designed to be used alone—without a diaphragm. These have shown effective dispersal and activity. In this respect they compare favorably with the foams, but have a tendency to be somewhat messier. Thus there may be some leakage, and the cream may disperse over areas adjacent to the genitals, including even the upper thighs. Some husbands, too, may object to a similar dispersal of the material over the shaft of the penis. On the other hand, there may be some comfort in actually seeing that the contraceptive cream is present, and where natural moisture is scanty the lubricating function may be of value. Only infrequently are there complaints of slight irritative reactions to the creams, such as burning or stinging. Since the products of different manufacturers vary in this respect, a shift to another brand may be desirable if any irritation is noted.

As with the foams, the creams are dispensed by use of a measuring device consisting of a plastic reservoir that attaches to the tube containing the contraceptive cream. A measured amount is delivered into the plastic container. The container is then inserted into the vagina as far as it will go, withdrawn approximately half an inch (to insure that some will be delivered around the cervix) and the material is than extruded. Although these contraceptive creams cling to the vaginal walls quite well, some leakage is bound to occur. Hence the following precautions should be taken:

1) If more than an hour has passed since insertion of the cream, the dose should be repeated. A second dose should also be administered in case intercourse is repeated.

2) If after inserting the cream one has to get up to walk around or go to the bathroom, and then goes back to bed, a second dose should be given. This will bring the total quantity in the vagina up to the needed level if, as is likely, some has been lost by activity.

3) Just as with the diaphragm and jelly techniques or with the foam, douching should be avoided for at least six hours after insertion of a cream. Since the creams are harmless, there is no specific need for douching in any event.

As between creams and jellies, the former seem to have the edge for effectiveness. The jellies appear to disperse somewhat more slowly. Since their basic constituents are often the same, the major difference is only that of the rate of dispersal. Direct observations have shown that sometimes a blob of the jelly may remain partially undispersed after insertion. Although theoretically further dispersal should take place with intercourse, if ejaculation occurs early this may not prove to be the case.

A similar criticism can be made of vaginal contraceptive suppositories. These are not to be confused with the various medicated suppositories prescribed for the treatment of many infections or vaginal inflammations. While some medicated suppositories might have agents damaging to sperm, they are not primarily contraceptive in action nor can they be used for this purpose. Only one vaginal suppository for contraceptive purposes has been approved by the Food and Drug Administration. Because of less even dispersal, it is regarded as inferior to the creams and foams. At least fifteen minutes must be allowed for melting and dispersal under the best of circumstances. As with other similar materials, another contraceptive suppository has to be inserted if a second intercourse occurs, or if after the original insertion the woman gets up to go to the bathroom or walks about, with resulting leakage. As with the jellies, creams, and foams, all of these agents are best inserted when the woman is lying down. In the case of the suppository, it should be tucked up as high as it can go, and at least fifteen minutes allowed to elapse for the cocoa butter or gelatin base to melt.

To sum up: as indicated elsewhere (Chapter 9) it is only recently that observations have been made on the use of these agents during simulated or actual intercourse. It is probable, provided all precautions are followed, that the best of the foams and creams will prove to have an excellent contraceptive efficiency. They do not rank as high as barrier methods such as the diaphragm and the condom and are certainly inferior to the pill. However, in certain combinations—i.e., condom plus foam, or cream plus rhythm method, etc.—a very high order of contraceptive efficiency should result. For women who cannot use the pill, such combinations offer the most reasonable alternatives.

Foams, Creams, and Jellies

The American Medical Association, which has taken an increasing interest in the necessity for disseminating information on birth control methods to its physician members, published in its journal (Oct. 25, 1965) an important listing of the various creams and foams in terms of their germ-killing efficiency. As may be seen, Delfen and Emko foams and Delfen cream were given the highest rating. The A.M.A. listing of these agents in decreasing order of efficiency is as follows: (the bracketed items are of similar efficiency, but there is a considerable difference between those at the top and those at the bottom).

VAGINAL FOAMS

Delfen Vaginal Foam,° Ortho Pharmaceutical Corp., Raritan, N.J.

Emko Vaginal Foam,° Emko Co., St. Louis

CREAMS AND JELLIES

Delfen Cream,° Ortho Pharmaceutical Corp., Raritan, N.J.

Certane Creme, Vogarell Products Co., Los Angeles
Contra Creme, Research Supplies, Albany, N.Y.

Creemoz Creme, Larré Labs., Division of Gynecic Laboratories, Inc., Yonkers, N.Y.
Lactikol Jelly, Durex Products, Inc., New York
Koromex-A Jelly,° Holland-Rantos Co., Inc., New York

Ortho-Gynol Jelly, Ortho Pharmaceutical Corp., Raritan, N.J.

Koromex-A Jelly, Holland-Rantos Co., Inc., New York
Marvosan Jelly, Veritas Products Co., Inc., Hillside, N.J.
Preceptin Gel,° Ortho Pharmaceutical Corp., Raritan, N.J.
Verithol Jelly, Veritas Products Co., Inc., Hillside, N.J.

Certane Jelly, Vogarell Products Co., Los Angeles
Lactikol Creme, Durex Products, Inc., New York
Ortho Creme, Ortho Pharmaceutical Corp., Raritan, N.J.

Immolin Cream-Jel,° Julius Schmid, Inc., New York
Koromex Cream, Holland-Rantos Co., Inc., New York
Locorol "D" Jelly,° Peck & Sterva Division, Inc., International Labs., Inc., Rochester, N.Y.

Lanesta Gel,° Esta Medical Labs., Inc., New York

° Products advertised or designed for use without mechanical (occlusive) protection.

Colagyn Jel,° The Smith Laboratory, Inc., Kansas City, Mo.
Lanteen Jelly, Esta Medical Labs., Inc., New York
Ramses Jelly, Julius Schmid, Inc., New York

Bilco Jelly, Veritas Products Co., Inc., Hillside, N.J.
Cooper Creme,° Whittaker Laboratories, Inc., Peeksville, N.Y.
Cooper Creme Gel, Whittaker Laboratories, Inc., Peekskill, N.Y.
Jellak Jelly, Larré Labs., Division of Gynecic Laboratories, Inc., Yonkers, N.Y.
Kemi-Cream, Kemi Products Corp., Clifton, N.J.
Kemi Jelly, Kemi Products Corp., Clifton, N.J.
Locorol Jelly, Peck & Sterba Division, Inc., International Labs., Inc., Rochester, N.Y.
Marvosan Creme, Veritas Products Co., Inc., Hillside, N.J.
Milex Crescent Creme, Milex Products, Chicago
Milex Crescent Jelly, Milex Products, Chicago
Milex Jelly B4,° Milex Products, Chicago
Veritas Kreme,° Veritas Products Co., Inc., Hillside, N.J.

VAGINAL FOAMING TABLETS

Durafoam Tablets,° Durex Products, Inc., New York
Zeptabs,° Larré Labs., Division of Gynecic Laboratories, Inc., Yonkers, N.Y.

SPONGE AND FOAM

Durafoam Liquid with Sponge, Durex Products, Inc., New York
Durex Foam Powder with Sponge, Durex Poducts, Inc., New York

VAGINAL SUPPOSITORIES

Lorophyn,° Eaton Laboratories, Norwich, N.Y.

° Products advertised or designed for use without mechanical (occlusive) protection.

7.
The Pill

Sᴇʟᴅᴏᴍ ʜᴀs ᴀɴʏ ɴᴇᴡ drug caught on as rapidly and met with such enthusiastic response as the birth control pills, often referred to collectively as "the pill." The drug was first introduced around 1957 by the Searle Company under the trade name of Enovid, but various changes in the original formulation have since been made. The low-dosage Enovid pill currently being used is quite different in its composition from the original one. In the past few years a number of other pills have been put on the market: Ortho Novum and Norinyl (the same drug under two different names), Provest, C-quens, Oracon, Ovulen; and there are new ones in the offing, to be introduced shortly.

It is estimated that at least five million women take a birth control pill every day in the United States. In Australia, where the pills have received even greater acceptance, one-third of the women of reproductive age are controlling their fertility by this means. Originally rather expensive, the cost of the pill has gone down until a month's supply runs in the range of $2.00, a series of price reductions having been made possible by changes in the formula plus increasing competition. Doubtless these price reductions are among the factors that have contributed to the widespread acceptance of the pill.

As is generally true whenever a new and important drug is introduced, reservations and doubts have been expressed by conservative doctors; and the pill has suffered from some adverse publicity since its appearance on the scene. Nonetheless it continues to be the contraceptive method which is most rapidly growing in acceptance in the United States, and for many good reasons.

Foremost among these is the fact that the pill is the best contraceptive agent available, bar none. Its efficacy seems unquestioned. When taken as directed, on a daily basis for twenty days, the pregnancy rate becomes approximately zero, a degree of effectiveness unmatched by any other known method. In addition to the formidable advantage of total effectiveness, the pill has many other features calculated to win consumer acceptance. There is no need to fumble around with mechanical devices of one sort or another. Lovemaking does not have to be interrupted while either the man or the woman dons suitable protection. No messy jelly or cream, to be used with or without a barrier device, is necessary. Nor is there any need to check the calendar to decide whether or not one can have marital relations, as adherents of the safe period must do. Clearly then, from the psychological and esthetic points of view, the advantages are all with the pill. Small wonder therefore that at planned parenthood centers, where various methods are described and offered, a majority of the women now select the pill as their first choice in contraception.

Despite all these clearcut advantages, the fact remains that the pill, which consists of new synthetic hormones and is a product of man's ingenuity in attempting to outwit nature, has led more than one disinterested critic to question whether this kind of hormonal tampering may not lead to difficulties which cannot at the present time be foreseen. And it must be admitted at the outset that not all of the questions raised have been answered definitively or satisfactorily. As is true with any new drug, the possibility of untoward consequences deserves thoughtful consideration: until a greater number of years have passed, an element of risk, however slight, doubtless does remain. But since we now have some ten years' experience with the use of the pill in one form or another, some reasonably educated guesses can be made, although another decade or two must pass before all the answers are in. To understand some of the pros and cons that have been raised, you should have a certain amount of knowledge as to how the pill works and what taking it month in, month out, implies.

How the Pill Works

The reasoning that led to the concept of the pill was both brilliant and simple. It was patterned on the course of events nature herself follows in every pregnancy, when ovulation and menstrual cycles are inhibited for the duration. Painstaking analysis of the reasons why women did not ovulate during pregnancy had shown that the basic cause was the failure of the pituitary gland to stimulate the ovary into a new cycle of activity. The pituitary, as we saw, is the master gland controlling the entire cycle of growth in the ovary, including the liberation of the egg cell. If the pituitary is not active, or is made inactive—which is what the birth control pill does—then there is a suspension of ovarian activity, and infertility results. The pituitary-ovary situation is comparable to the relationship between the motor and the wheels of the automobile. If the motor cannot be fired up, the wheels will not move.

119

Sex, Fertility, and Birth Control

It had long been known from examination of the ovaries of pregnant women during emergency abdominal operations that there were no new follicles and no evidence of ovulation taking place during the nine months of gestation. What inactivated the pituitary during all this time? It was found that this inactivation of the pituitary—and hence, of the whole cycle—resulted from the great outpouring of hormones from the placenta (afterbirth) which begins soon after the fertilized egg burrows into the uterine lining. This hormonal outpouring from an endocrine organ, peculiar to pregnancy, is in essence a message to the pituitary gland stating that with so much in the way of female hormones being produced, there is no further need for pituitary activity in this area. Consequently, normal production of pituitary hormones capable of stimulating the ovary into a new cycle of growth is inhibited. No new egg cells can therefore mature.

A pregnant woman is literally flooded with both estrogen and progestin, the two hormones secreted by the ovary in a normal cycle. The first birth control pills were calculated to duplicate this effect and thus to secure the same inactivation of the pituitary. Both hormones had been available since the early 1930's; the drawback was that the forms then available had to be injected—they were not active when taken by mouth, and the taking of frequent injections to prevent ovulation, while theoretically a possibility, was hardly practical. However, this barrier was successfully breached when chemical compounds were synthesized which possessed many of the properties of the naturally produced hormones, with the added important advantage that they could be successfully taken by mouth. The appearance of these new orally active compounds made the birth control pill possible.

All of the original birth control pills tended to mimic pregnancy to some degree. Thus the changes in the breasts and the lining of the uterus were similar to those found in

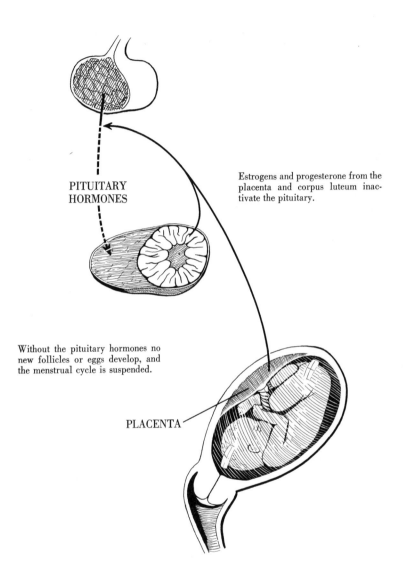

PITUITARY
HORMONES

Estrogens and progesterone from the placenta and corpus luteum inactivate the pituitary.

Without the pituitary hormones no new follicles or eggs develop, and the menstrual cycle is suspended.

PLACENTA

FIGURE 17

a pregnant woman. Indeed, some of the complaints made by users of the pill had a familiar ring to the obstetrician, for they duplicated the discomforts that pregnant women mention, including nausea, weight gain, swelling of the breasts, fluid retention, and sometimes psychic disturbances. Particularly with the early versions of the pill, where dosages were unnecessarily large, all these undesirable effects—termed side effects—troubled a considerable percentage of users. In fact, 5 to 10 per cent of the women taking pills found the side effects so troublesome that they abandoned this form of contraception altogether.

Fortunately, experimentation with different dosages showed that the hormonal ingredients of the early pills could be cut substantially. Lowering the dosage, as well as use of new forms of the agents, eventually led to fewer complaints about side effects. Thus in the oldest of this series of pills, Enovid, the dose of synthetic progestin was ultimately cut to only one-fourth of that originally used. Recently, in another important modification, physicians have been giving only one of the hormones throughout most of the artificial cycle, then the combination for a final five-day period. This method is known as the sequential pill, two versions of which are the Upjohn Company's Oracon and the Lilly Company's C-quens. With these, as with certain other versions of the birth control pill currently under investigation, it is possible to expect still further lessening of side effects.

A recent, unreleased form of the pill has been further simplified and works on another principle altogether—its mechanism of action is itself different. It contains only one hormone, does not inhibit ovulation, and appears to work by changing the cervical mucus so that the sperm cannot ascend.

Despite the continued improvements in the formulation of the pill, a few women continue to have annoying problems with it, one of the most common being spotting or staining. This condition, which comes on irregularly while the pill is being taken and may require the wearing of a napkin, is called breakthrough bleeding (BTB). Its exact cause is not known. It is more common during the first few cycles during which the pill is used, and sometimes merely increasing the dosage or shifting to another pill solves the BTB problem. With most women, it is quite easy to distinguish between BTB and a menstrual period. However, if BTB is heavy or persistent it may simulate a period —in fact, if the pill is discontinued because of it, the extent of BTB increases and what seems to be a typical flow may follow. In most instances of BTB, the same or another brand of pill may be taken in a succeeding cycle with reasonable expectation of avoiding a repetition of the bleeding. However, some women have so much of a problem with it that they give up use of the pill altogether. Contrariwise, the pill may have a welcome effect on menstrual bleeding. Thus some women who have had many heavy periods with prolonged flow are surprised and delighted to find their flow becoming shorter and scantier. Often painful cramps are diminished or even disappear altogether. In fact, the pills have been used to secure these results where no contraceptive need as such existed.

The method of taking the pills is simplicity itself, and their manufacturers vie with one another to see who can show more ingenuity in making the procedure simplest and most readily understandable. The normal menstrual cycle is imitated to such a degree that the woman who goes on the pill can expect to have regularly recurring menstrual periods every 28 days. The generalized directions for taking pills are as follows:

1. In all instances, 20 pills are to be taken in each menstrual cycle.

2. The first day of menstruation being Day 1 of the cycle, the first pill is taken on Day 5, whether or not menstruation has ceased. Thus if one has a menstrual flow start-

ing on a Monday, the first birth control pill would be taken that Friday.

3. Thereafter a pill is taken each day, preferably at the same time—this can be in the morning, in the evening, or at any other suitable time—for the next 20 days. Most often the pills are dispensed in a grouping of 20, and they may be numbered accordingly.

4. After the 20 pills have been taken in the 20 days, they are discontinued. Generally a menstrual flow will begin within two or three days. This may be somewhat different from the usual flow the woman has experienced, but not necessarily. The onset of the menstrual flow marks a new cycle: Day 1 of that cycle is ushered in.

5. The pills are resumed on Day 5 of the succeeding cycle. The process can be repeated cycle after cycle.

In the great majority of women—well over 90 per cent —the pills work beautifully. As has already been suggested, a few problems may be encountered, especially during the first several cycles. If such problems do arise, it is occasionally necessary to modify the routine instructions. Thus, if a woman complains of nausea, it may be recommended that the pill be divided in half and taken in two doses instead of all at once; or it may be taken at night before retiring; or specific instructions may be given to take it following the largest meal of the the day, usually dinner. If breakthrough bleeding occurs, the physician may advise doubling the dose for a few days, during which time the spotting may clear up. A few women have found that with some versions of the pill their usual menstrual period does not occur after the full course of 20 pills have been taken. If no bleeding has occurred by the seventh day after stopping the pills, and if this is the first cycle in which failure to menstruate has occurred, it is generally suggested that the course of pills be repeated. If failure to menstruate occurs again, a different pill may be tried in the next cycle. Then again, a woman who is already pregnant without knowing it, may start on the pills, whereupon the anticipated flow does not result because of the unsuspected pregnancy. It is therefore wise, whenever the pills are not working as they are supposed to, to check with the doctor.

Although many women feel fine when pregnant, a few do not. By the same token, some users of birth control pills may experience vague psychological changes and sub-par feelings. Thus a few women report being edgy, nervous, or somewhat depressed while on one or another version of the pill. Others suffer from light-headedness or other vague "off" feelings, and still others from minor digestive complaints such as bloating, "gasiness," or constipation. Finally, a few, especially those women likely to have headaches about the time of their periods, have also complained of headache while on the pill.

Since the pills are so new, all the reports dealing with them have attempted to be objective, listing all of the complaints made by any and all of the subjects taking them. There is no doubt that this in a way does injustice to the pill, for the implication is that whatever complaints a woman may have during the months she is on the medication are attributed to it. But the fact is that few adults can go through any six-month period without at one time or another noticing such sensations as headache, sub-par feelings, tiredness, perhaps even weight gain or digestive disturbances. It is also an unquestioned fact, demonstrated in many studies, that a considerable number of individuals observe changes in themselves even when they take an inert medication. A sugar capsule, for example, has been known to produce such symptoms as nausea, headache, dizziness, weakness, and digestive disturbances. Conversely, sugar pills have been reported to cure headache, alleviate nausea and dizziness, and produce an increased sense of well-being. All these effects, both negative and positive, observed when a person takes an inert medicine, are termed "placebo effects." They are not imaginary: they seem to be real changes occurring within the person as a result of the suggestive power of swallowing a pill, *any* pill. Thus many of the untoward side effects reported by users of the contraceptive pill fall into this category and are similar to the findings invariably reported on investigation of any new drug. This is not to deny that the pills are potent medication, that they do change the hormonal balance within the body, and that some of their users' vaguer or less well-defined complaints are unquestionably related to the hormonal changes produced. But one should not jump to hasty conclusions.

Since the body has a capacity to develop tolerance for many medications, many of the genuine side effects produced by the pill tend to disappear after several cycles. Hence women who continue to use them in spite of the discomforts report a decreasing number of side effects after a few months, with the remaining ones seemingly diminishing in intensity. The situation may be likened to the tolerance the body develops for so common a habit as smoking. The dizziness, nausea, or rapid heartbeat which the novice develops when smoking his first cigarette disappears if he persists in this bad habit. Similar tolerances develop for coffee, alcohol, sleeping pills, and a large number of other agents.

In general it may be said that the side effects of the pill are tolerable, and that tolerance will almost certainly develop. It has been estimated, therefore, that about 95 per cent of women in their reproductive years could use the pill as a contraceptive method without significant drawbacks. However, the birth control pill is not for all women in all circumstances. Just as some people cannot tolerate valuable drugs like penicillin or aspirin, some women may not tolerate the pill. The reason may be either some condition which existed in the past, or a currently existing one. Among these are the following:

1. *Fibroids.* Fibroids are benign growths on the uterine

muscular wall. They are often multiple, and can lead to a bumpy irregular enlargement of the uterus. Perhaps half of all women develop at least a few small fibroids. These may become quite large and even exert pressure on such adjacent organs as the bladder. They may also be responsible for an irregular or prolonged menstrual flow. It has been observed that already existing fibroids may increase in growth rate when birth control pills are used: hence women with significant fibroids are advised against the use of the pill as a contraceptive method.

2. *History of vein clots or inflammation.* The formation of a clot in a vein, especially in the lower extremities or in the pelvis, is by no means rare. It is sometimes observed after a blow to a vein. More often it seems to occur spontaneously and has been ascribed to the sluggish flow of blood that occurs in the great veins, plus perhaps an increased tendency of the blood to coagulate or clot. Sometimes the vein in which the clot occurs becomes tender and inflamed, a condition known as phlebitis. Danger arises when a portion of such a clot breaks off and moves on to an important organ such as the lungs. Trapping of the clot in an organ such as the lung can lead to a serious consequence—pulmonary embolism. Clotting in the tiny blood vessels of the eyes may impair sight.

It is an everyday observation that some people clot more readily—just as some bleed more readily—than others, the ready clotting being quite possibly due to some inherent tendency. There has therefore been a good deal of discussion pro and con as to whether the birth control pill might conceivably increase this tendency. However, it has been extremely difficult to ascertain whether users of the pill actually do experience more clots than non-users: innumerable studies of the blood-clotting mechanisms seem to indicate little or no change in the many constituents involved in clot formation. Clots can of course occur spontaneously in women who never used the pill. Many thousands of cases of blood clots in women between the ages of twenty and forty were recorded long before the pills were even invented. The controversy now is whether frequency of clotting has or has not increased with use of the pill.

In 1962, at the instigation of the Federal Government, a special committee led by a distinguished authority in the area, Dr. Irving Wright, critically reviewed all of the data on this subject and concluded that there was no increased risk of thrombosis and embolism with use of Enovid. Although the report made by this committee was subsequently criticized on several grounds, certainly if any increased risk does exist it is very hard to demonstrate and must accordingly be very small indeed.

Is the Pill Dangerous?

The pharmaceutical explosion of recent years has made medicine richer and wiser—richer because it has extended the range of diseases and conditions which the doctor can treat; wiser because it has taught that drugs are potent agents, to be administered thoughtfully and with caution, and that all drug therapy can be a two-edged sword. Gone indeed are the days when drugs were simple, their action readily understood, and their safety backed by decades if not centuries of experience.

The questions so often raised as to the safety of birth control pills—especially their long-range safety—are therefore quite understandable. In addition to the fears regarding alteration in the incidence of cancer or of clotting, it has been argued that one should not tinker with such glands as the pituitary and the ovary, that one should not introduce new hormones into the body because of the complex interrelations between these glands, and that in general no one can predict what might be the long-range impact of synthetic hormonal agents.

Several other bugaboos and some idle though interesting speculations have been raised ever since the advent of the pill. One is that with ovulation prevented month after month and year after year, users might experience delayed menopause (change of life). There was even some speculation that women might retain fertility into their sixties and seventies because their reproductive life had been prolonged. The fact of the matter is, however, that in women who have had multiple pregnancies, a condition in many respects similar to the situation that is created while the pills are taken, the menopause appears at the usual time, so that there seems to be no basis for assuming the pill has any bearing on the problem.

Another, more serious question has been raised as to the possible effect of the pill on cancer of the breasts and reproductive tract. Cancers of the breasts and of the uterus are far and away the most common of all malignant tumors in women, so that even a very slight tendency toward an increase would potentially affect thousands of persons. Some authorities feel there is just as much reason to expect a decrease in the incidence of cancer with use of the pill. Final answers to these and many other questions can come only with prolonged observation and study carried on over many years. The best we can say for the time being is that, so far, the group of women in Puerto Rico who have been observed over the past seven or more years seem to show a *lessened incidence* of cancer than might have been anticipated. If this fascinating preliminary observation is verified, we may witness a scramble on the part of women everywhere to use the pill as a prophylactic measure against the development of cancer—a vastly different situation indeed from what was originally suggested and feared.

Yet it must be admitted that no one can speak with total assurance about the long-term safety of the birth control pills. At the present time the Food and Drug Administration insists that manufacturers enclose a long and detailed statement with all literature and samples of the pill distributed to doctors, including a list of all the possible side effects and many of the adverse observations made to date. Recommendations are made that the drug not be used for more than two to four years, in a few instances a little longer. One of the thoughts behind this admonition is that a new pill, even if demonstrated to have no untoward effects over the relatively brief two- or four-year span, may not be unreservedly endorsed for use over a period of five or seven years, perhaps longer. Nonetheless, some woman are already known to have been taking the first or later versions of birth control pills for six, seven, or even more years with no evidence of any complications. Also, some of the fears originally expressed regarding the long-term effect of the pill have already been resolved. Thus the fear that there might be some interference with fertility when a woman taking the pills decides to become pregnant has been proved groundless. Women who stop using birth control pills are almost immediately fertile. Indeed, some studies seem to indicate they become pregnant quicker than the women in control groups; and their offspring are entirely normal.

In medicine, it is not always wise to reason from analogy; but perhaps the analogy to the common administration of thyroid may hold for the pill. The reciprocal relationship between the pituitary and thyroid glands is the same as that between the pituitary and the ovary. Now the fact is that thyroid extract has been widely—and often indiscriminately—prescribed for thousands of patients. At one time almost any woman complaining of irregular or prolonged menstrual periods or difficulty in becoming pregnant, as well as women complaining of lack of pep, a tendency to gain weight, or even dry skin or thin hair, were likely be given thyroid pills. Many of the pills used in the treatment of that most widespread of all conditions, obesity, also contained thyroid. When thyroid is thus taken, there is a prompt drop in the secretion of the individual's own thyroid gland. This drop in the activity of the patient's own thyroid will last so long as the thyroid pills are being taken. When thyroid administration is stopped, the old relationship between the pituitary and the thyroid gland reasserts itself; the thyroid is stimulated into more activity, and within a few weeks returns to its old former level of secretion.

Thyroid pills have been prescribed and swallowed literally by the hundred million tablets. There is no evidence whatsoever that this somewhat indiscriminate, free-and-easy taking of the medication has had any adverse long-term effect on either the thyroid gland itself or on its controlling gland, the pituitary. All observations so far indicate that the same situation will hold with the taking of the birth control pills. In other words, there will be an absence of ovarian activity while a woman is taking the pills, then a resumption of activity by the pituitary and the ovary when she stops taking them. Indeed, some evidence seems to indicate a swing of the pendulum in the opposite direction, in that women who have been on the pill for some time may be more fertile than normal once they go off it.

The chemical composition of the ingredients of the pill is not such as to indicate impending danger. One of the components, estrogen, falls into a category of compounds that have been prescribed for many years to women during their menopause, as well as women whose own ovarian performance has for one reason or another been inadequate. The long-term effects of estrogen on the reproductive organs or other organs of the body indicate that, as with the hormone manufactured by the woman's own ovary, new, unexpected, or unforseeable damage does not occur. The second hormone contained in the pills, a synthetic progestin, is one about which less is known; but, again, the accumulated body of knowledge dealing with substances in this category indicates little if any probability of an untoward or completely unexpected abnormal reaction. In short, the compounds contained in the birth control pills are not completely

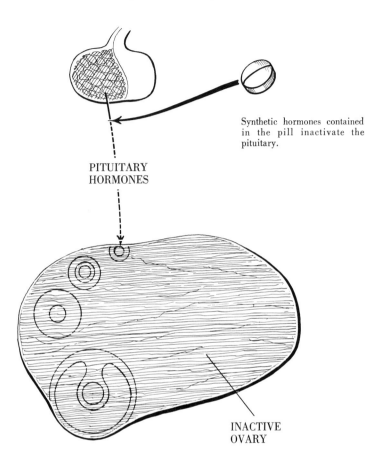

Synthetic hormones contained in the pill inactivate the pituitary.

PITUITARY
HORMONES

INACTIVE
OVARY

Without the pituitary hormones, no new follicles develop, and there is no ovulation. Without follicular growth and without formation of the corpus luteum, the ovary does not produce estrogen or progesterone. By the action of hormones supplied by the pill, menstrual cycles are continued.

FIGURE 18

strange, completely new chemicals, but rather fall into categories of substances with which there is long-standing familiarity backed by a considerable body of knowledge.

It is to be remembered in this connection that there is no such thing as a drug which is *completely* safe, irrespective of how it is used. Too much aspirin can produce digestive symptoms varying from heartburn or upset stomach to serious bleeding. One or two cocktails a day can be fine for producing relaxation and improving the circulation, but large amounts of alcohol can damage the liver, produce acute inflammation of the pancreas, and even ruin the brain. Compared to what alcohol can do to some individuals, one might argue that the birth control pills obviously fall into a less risky category.

We might best sum it up as follows: There is some inherent risk in the taking of drugs—any drugs. This holds for birth control pills as much as for numerous other freely dispensed medications which are taken without creating undue anxiety. Perhaps there are some minimal risks inherent in taking the pill; but the level of risk at the present time is so small that for practical purposes it can be disregarded. With some individuals who fall into special groupings, it would certainly be prudent to avoid taking the pill, and such persons will doubtless be so informed by their doctor. To recapitulate, this would include women with a past history of clotting in the veins, of liver disease, tumors of the reproductive tract, perhaps diabetes, and a few individuals with other diseases.

But in general the average woman who elects to take the pill has no reason to hesitate about its use on the basis of present knowledge. Where the pill is acceptable, its 100-per-cent effectiveness as a contraceptive certainly gives it a unique appeal. This fact, plus the esthetic acceptability of the device, the simplicity with which it can be used, and its constantly diminishing cost all account for the phenomenal increase in its acceptance and popularity.

8.
Intrauterine Contraceptive Devices (IUCD)

THERE IS GREAT EXCITEMENT in many important world circles over a series of new devices with a potential for the greatest impact on the population problem. Despite their relatively recent introduction, these devices have captured the attention of many of the governments of underdeveloped countries faced with the explosive consequences of population expansion. These are a group of devices, made mostly of plastic, a few of metal or other materials, which are inserted directly into the uterus. Collectively they are known as intrauterine contraceptive devices or IUCD's (also IUD's) for short. It has not yet been finally determined what the most effective size and shape for one of these devices should be. A variety of them are still under active investigation, and doubtless new and perhaps odder forms may appear. Some are shaped like the coils of a snail's shell; another is a loop which looks like two S's one on top of the other; still another, the bow, has the shape of a bow tie.

The IUCD's may yet turn out to be the most important contribution of the Age of Plastics. Being made of plastic, they are cheap and easily manufactured on a large-scale basis; and because of their inherent flexibility they are also a good deal easier to insert into the uterus than the metal ones. Thus even a wide contorted plastic device can be uncoiled into a long strand, readily placed inside a narrow inserter, then conveyed into the uterus. Once the inserter is removed, the stretched plastic device assumes its former shape—a series of coils or loops or the like.

So far none of these devices has been wholly satisfactory, but the intense effort focused on them makes continued improvement likely. The chief reason for the intense interest in them is that when it works, the IUCD has many of the characteristics of a perfect contraceptive. Here are some of the important positive features of IUCD's:

1. Once inserted and retained, the IUCD acts as a contraceptive month after month without further attention.
2. The devices appear to be safe. There are no significant local effects on the tissues from the presence of the plastic device.
3. With a successful IUCD there is no further need for preparation for intercourse, no purchase of new supplies of medication, no need to return to the physician for checkups, no need for slipping the device in and out as with the diaphragm and cap.
4. There is no impairment of fertility because of the device. When the IUCD's are removed, more than 80 per cent of users become pregnant within a year—which is about the expected rate.

Particularly in the underdeveloped countries, the IUCD has looked like the answer to married women's prayers and to the impossible population pressures faced by desperate governments. In those lands, experience with the compli-

INTRAUTERINE CONTRACEPTIVE DEVICES

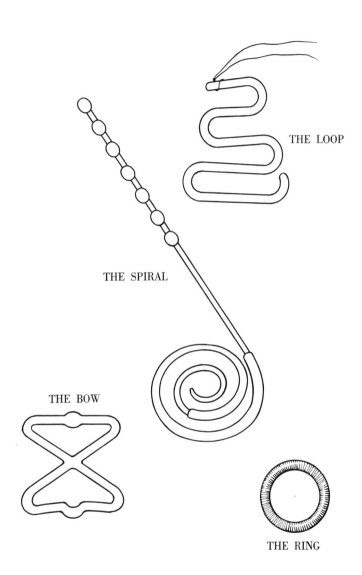

THE LOOP

THE SPIRAL

THE BOW

THE RING

FIGURE 19

cated, sophisticated, or expensive methods used in Europe and the United States has emphasized all sorts of practical difficulties. The pill with its admirable efficiency rate of virtually 100 per cent is relatively expensive, must be taken daily, the days of the cycle must be reckoned, and supplies renewed. The diaphragm requires instruction, supervision, an initial fitting by a physician, and a new fitting from time to time during a woman's reproductive life. Since with less than well-motivated couples intercourse may occur without preliminary insertion of the diaphragm, among uncooperative or the less educated groups the failure rate is considerably higher than is reported for women visiting United States Planned Parenthood Centers. The cervical cap, widely used in Europe, generally calls for fairly frequent visits to the doctor, and this too is an impossibility in the underdeveloped countries.

Because of its manifest advantages, the IUCD has received unprecedented acceptance in many parts of the world. As a result, despite its comparatively recent introduction, a considerable body of data concerning it is already available. All of the preliminary results seem to be so favorable from the point of view of mass population control that insertion of IUCD's is going on at an unprecedented rate. In fact, in some of the countries where the population problem is a critical one, nonmedical personnel is being trained to handle its distribution so that even the most outlying villages can be supplied with it. The devices are thus made available to everyone, and inserted then and there.

This considerable degree of acceptance in all parts of the world does not by any means imply that the IUCD's are free of significant drawbacks. The drawbacks are such that perhaps only 80 per cent of the women who have been fitted with them will be able to retain and profit from them on a long-term basis. Perhaps the percentage of women who can tolerate the present crop of IUCD's will increase as time goes on and new designs are created and introduced. At present, the following are some of the important difficulties that have been noted:

1. *Expulsion of the device.* With one of the best-studied of the IUCD's, the Lippes loop, there is approximately a 10 per cent incidence of expulsion. Perhaps the most common time for it to be expelled is at menstruation. When expulsion does occur, it is generally suggested that a new, perhaps slightly larger IUCD be inserted—possibly more than once—before all attempts to use the device are abandoned. Some women seem to be more prone to expulsion of the device than others. Sometimes an IUCD of somewhat different shape rather than of different size may be retained better than a smaller one of the same design.

2. *Spotting and bleeding.* It is not uncommon for some bleeding to occur after a device has been inserted. In a small percentage of women—perhaps 2 per cent—continued spotting or bleeding may make it necessary to remove the device.

3. *Pain.* In a small percentage of women, the IUCD produces pain quite similar to menstrual cramps. This is sometimes associated with spotting. Oddly enough, some women report relief of menstrual cramps after an IUCD has been inserted.

4. *Inflammations.* The presence of a foreign body in the uterus with or without an extension down through the canal of the cervix may sometimes lead to inflammation or infection. Doubtless in some of the reported cases a low-grade infection was already present and was made more acute by the manipulation necessary for installing the device. Where a woman has a previous history of infections of the reproductive tract, it may be wise not to use an IUCD.

The problem of unnoticed expulsion, of course, creates difficulties from a contraceptive viewpoint. Devices can be expelled without the woman being aware of it, and only when an unwanted pregnancy occurs is the absence of the device discovered. Most of the devices are expelled during the first month (particularly, as we have said, at the time of the menstrual period), and women should be instructed to keep this possibility in mind. To help get around this, some of the devices have a built-in arrangement which makes it easy to determine whether they are being retained. The spiral device, for example, has a long, beaded plastic tail which runs down through the cervical canal and protrudes into the vagina. At the time of insertion the protruding tail is clipped down to size. There is thus left a small protuberance which can readily be felt or seen and assures one that the device is still in place. Still another of the successful devices, the loop, has two nylon threads which also are allowed to protrude through the cervical canal.

Both the plastic tail and the nylon threads make removal of the device easy, a further important advantage. Otherwise a blunt hooklike device must be inserted by the doctor when removal of an ICUD is desired. It has been argued that the presence of a protruding plastic tail or similar extension from the uterus down to the vagina may predispose to ascending infection. Although this may sometimes occur, infection has not been as significant as had at first been anticipated. Indeed what has been surprising has been the inertness of the plastics—despite the continued presence of a foreign body month after month, there is little or no evidence of inflammation. There has been one unforeseen difficulty with the protruding plastic tail of the Margulies spiral: in a few cases there have been complaints from husbands that they can feel this tip when having intercourse. This situation is easily remedied by cutting down on the length of the tail, so that it is made just about flush with the tip end of the cervix.

When there is no protruding tip or threads to an IUCD, one may not be sure that the device is still within the uterus except by taking an X ray. The plastic devices or the stainless steel ring are easily seen on such an X ray. There is considerable reassurance value to both patient and doctor when they can tell, either by feeling or looking, that the IUCD is still in place. A further advantage with models having nylon threads or similar extensions is that the device can be removed by a woman herself, if necessary, as when she decides that she wants to try for a pregnancy. Accordingly some of the older plastic models are now appearing with nylon threads added.

How do the IUCD's work? There is no interference either with ovulation or with the upward journey of sperm. The uterine lining goes through its usual changes during the cycle, with little or no alteration that could be ascribed to the inlying plastic device. On the other hand, there is some evidence that it may hasten the transit of the egg through the tube. This tubal journey, during which the fertilized egg goes through repeated multiplications, thus forming a little ball of cells, normally takes three days. Possibly some acceleration of the journey through the tube brings it into the uterus before it is able to implant in normal fashion. Or it may be that unfavorable changes take place in the outermost cells lining the uterus, and that these changes repel the egg. Whatever the explanation, observations on many thousands of women in different parts of the world have established the IUCD as the most important recent advance in the field.

There are some failures, of course. A few pregnancies have occurred and proceeded normally for the nine-month period, resulting in a normal full-term baby, despite the continued presence of the intrauterine device. Moreover, the IUCD is not recommended for women who have never had a pregnancy, the reason for this being that insertion of the device requires dilation of the canal and more manipulation than is considered desirable in such cases. But this still leaves a great many women—those who have had as many babies as they want—eligible for a device which four-fifths of them can use indefinitely. It has been estimated that over 200,000 women in the United States have already had an IUCD inserted. What about the remainder? A major obstacle has been the newness of the device, many doctors objecting to the widespread use of any new method or drug. They feel that only the passage of time and a great deal of accumulated experience can give us sufficiently accurate data on the difficulties or hazards which a new advance of this kind may bring. The history of medicine is filled with innovations which were first hailed with enthusiasm and later shown to have unforeseen drawbacks. For instance, it took years to find out that the wonder drug penicillin produced sensitivity and severe reactions in more than 5 per cent of the population, and thus could not be prescribed indiscriminately.

When it comes to health matters, it is difficult to criticize cautious wait-and-see attitudes. But in justice to the IUCD it must be said that the experience with small groups of women who have been followed for a number of years all indicates that no unforeseen problems are likely to arise. Whatever difficulties the devices do present are most likely to be manifest within the first few months, not later.

The history of the IUCD's goes back to 1928, when Dr. Gräfenberg of Germany, using a steel ring at the time, reported on its value and effectiveness. Other doctors associated with him subsequently reported on the protracted use of IUCD's by women whose reactions were followed over some years. But despite these favorable reports the IUCD was virtually neglected by the medical profession, much as the original discovery of penicillin in 1929 was neglected for more than a decade. It can safely be said, however, that groups of women under observation for many years, after using a number of the older devices, have not shown any significant problem even with the passage of time.

It is also safe to predict that more will be heard about IUCD's, for their undoubted advantages remain beyond dispute. In the United States, a country where most of the population can afford birth control pills, fittings for diaphragms, or the purchase of condoms, where every household has a calendar and the average couple can be taught to cope with rhythm mathematics, IUCD's may lag behind other, better-established techniques. In the rest of the world the reverse will surely be the case. The reports quoted earlier from Taiwan, the fact that a recently opened factory in India is geared to manufacturing approximately five million plastic loops per year, the mass programs currently under way in Pakistan, Hong Kong, Chile, and the West Indies for insertion of IUCD's, and finally their rapid acceptance in other underdeveloped countries all seem to prove this. It is entirely possible that a modified intrauterine device with a greater retention rate may become the best-known and most widely used contraceptive of the future.

9.
Effect of Intercourse on Contraceptives

Considering the very nature of sexual intercourse and its everyday occurrence throughout the centuries, it is surprising how little has been known of the changes that occur with it in both sexes. Even such elementary and needed information as what intercourse does to the pulse and the blood pressure has been determined only relatively recently. The impact of sexual intercourse on contraceptive methods, including such mechanical barriers as the diaphragm and the cervical cap, has not been studied until the past half dozen years. This is admittedly a delicate area in which to collect information, but difficult is not the same as impossible. From time to time a few original minds have tackled the problem. It is perhaps worthy of note that one of the great geniuses of all times, Leonardo da Vinci, had a considerable interest in many aspects of human reproduction. In the course of his anatomical studies he studied the structure of the pregnant uterus. He also studied and drew other portions of the reproductive tract and left us with a remarkable drawing of human intercourse which he called the congress of the sexes. One is not likely to see it in any of our museums, and of course though drawn by one of the great masters, it ranks primarily as a medical illustration. To Leonardo, with his massive intellect and enormous curiosity, nothing that occurred on this earth would have been considered banned to inquiry or exploration. It is odd nonetheless that centuries were to pass before some of the subjects he dealt with—varying from sexual intercourse to the flying machine—were to be taken up anew.

In fact some of the most pertinent observations on sexual function, especially in women, have been sought for and described for the first time only in the past few years. Much of the new facts in this area we owe to the studies of Dr. William Masters and his group at Washington University School of Medicine. Their studies have uncovered much that is new in the sexual response of women and the effect that some of these observed changes may have on fertility and sterility. Many of the observations were made on groups of women volunteers who were studied throughout phases of sexual excitement and orgasm, and in whom simulated or actual intercourse was evaluated also as it might affect different contraceptive methods. These highly original investigations have certainly helped to explain some of the known variations in effectiveness of birth control techniques and for the first time give a dynamic picture of the female sexual responses.

The studies have shown that women participate in and respond very actively to sexual stimulation, and some of the alterations produced are of a quality and quantity previously unsuspected. Perhaps the field had been dominated too long by the assumption that it was the male that underwent the striking changes, such as erection, while the female was passively penetrated, a kind of vessel for acceptance of the sperm. The truth of the matter is that the female undergoes an engorgement and swelling in the pelvic region which is entirely comparable to that occurring in the male. In addition to marked congestion in the labia and vaginal opening, there are also a swelling and enlargement of the breasts and nipples and a rashlike mottling of the skin of the breasts and abdomen.

It has long been known that promptly with the onset of sexual stimulation in women a fluid secretion which acts as a vaginal lubricant begins to appear. The amount varies in different women and depends in part on the depth and prolongation of adequate sexual stimulation. For many years it was taught that this secretion came from Bartholin's glands, two glands immediately at the opening of the vagina, with perhaps part of the secretion also coming from the cervix. Dr. Masters' observations indicate quite clearly that cervical secretion is nonexistent, so that use of a diaphragm or cap would in no way interfere with lubrication for intercourse. Also the secretion from the Bartholin's glands is of relatively little importance and appears quite late. Instead, he made the surprising observation that as little as fifteen seconds after onset of sexual response fluid droplets begin to appear in amongst the folds of the vaginal lining. These little beads of secretion, for all the world like beads of sweat on the skin, increase in amount if the sex stimulus continues. There is finally a running together of the secretion which provides a uniformly distributed lubricant fluid.

A peculiarity of this sequence of events is that there are virtually no glands in the vagina and the observations fail to explain where the fluid comes from. It would appear that the droplets result from a leakage through the walls of vaginal blood vessels which become increasingly congested as the sexual response proceeds. It is doubtless of some importance in studies of fertility that such a secretion may tend to neutralize vaginal acidity. Vaginal acidity is known to be harmful to sperm, so that the vaginal lubricating fluid may play an important part in reducing the acidity of the area into which the sperm will be received.

With continuation of sexual stimulation, an intense congestive reaction progresses in the vaginal tissues, particularly that part of the vaginal barrel near the opening. This may have the net effect of actually narrowing the vaginal opening, a change which might be compared to the familiar narrowing in the airway of the nose produced when congestion of its lining occurs. (In fact the lining of the nose is classified as an erectile tissue, a tissue which expands greatly in size when its blood vessels fill up.) This swelling at the very vaginal gateway would have the net effect of more firmly encircling the penis. A similar congestion with swelling appears in the vaginal lips. The lesser lips, the labia minora, may swell to double their previous volume. Initially they appear pink, later turning a dusky red. In women who have had one or more pregnancies and in whom the blood vessels supplying the area have been modified, the labia minora may become a burgundy red in appearance. There are associated changes in the labia majora or outer lips also. These may either be passively pushed to either side by the swelling going on in the adjacent inner tissues or may also undergo swelling and expansion as part of the congestive reaction. All this congestion in the outer part of the vagina and the adjacent labia may in effect lengthen the canal for purposes of intercourse. These swollen tissues thus become a platform whereon many of the changes associated with the orgasm occur— the "orgasmic platform."

Equally marked and previously unsuspected changes are also occurring further up. There is a relaxation of the vaginal walls, so that the size of the area into which the semen is about to be delivered increases considerably. This ballooning expansion of the deep vaginal vault—the receptacle in which the semen can be pooled—is accompanied by a movement upward of the cervix and of the uterus, which now rises higher within the pelvis. All these changes are reversed reasonably promptly with orgasm, very slowly and incompletely in the absence of one. The orgasm itself is marked by intense throbbing muscular contractions felt in the vaginal opening and in the muscles about it. These involuntary contractions occur at approximately one-second intervals and half a dozen or more of them may be experienced. Orgasm may be associated with further involuntary pelvic thrusting motions and an almost complete blocking out of all other incoming sensations. Sights, sounds, pain, and other feelings may be dimmed or disappear in the course of the seizure that leads to the release of the orgasm.

Following the orgasm there is usually a great deal of relief from the previously mounting sexual tension. However, with some women continued sexual stimulation may be maintained and they can experience multiple orgasms in close succession. Otherwise there is a fairly rapid resolution of the many changes brought on by sexual excitement. These changes do proceed more slowly than the equivalent ones of the male. There is gradual decongestion of the engorged orgasmic platform over a period of some minutes. The inner end of the vagina narrows down and the cervix descends from its former elevated position. This descent theoretically would immerse it in the seminal pool deposited in the vagina and perhaps help conception. However, if orgasm is not experienced some of the congestive changes which persist act like a stopper. This would tend to favor retention of semen and hence the possibility of impregnation. From the viewpoint of impregnation, the plus and minus changes that occur with orgasm may cancel each other out. Certainly orgasm is not necessary for conception. Other factors are important. Thus retention of semen is favored by maintenance of the supine position, especially if the legs are drawn up (see Chapter 4).

Many of the changes that accompany the female sexual response show some variability from one woman to another. Some secrete more vaginal fluid than others, so that lubrication is a variable. The degree of congestion that occurs varies from slight to moderate to profound. It may even be variable in the same woman from one time to another, depending on factors such as the intensity of sexual stimulation. Other individual factors such as fatigue, perhaps also previous sexual experiences, and changes due to the menstrual cycle may all have some modifying influence. Some critics might doubtless say that women willing to volunteer for these experiments, in which they knew they would undergo observation, may have been different and respond differently than more modest, nonvolunteering ones. The subjects were picked because they generally had orgasms— sometimes repeatedly and frequently. Some, however, occationally failed to achieve orgasm.

There are, of course, a substantial minority of women who seldom or never experience an orgasm and others with quite indifferent attitudes towards sex. Doubtless many of them (as was true of some of the women in the Masters group on isolated occasions) undergo little of the usual congestive changes associated with stimulation. However, Dr. Masters' observations have been both sufficiently varied and repetitive so that one can be reasonably certain that what he has described is in fact the characteristic sexual response of the human female. Included in his group were women with varied reproductive backgrounds. Among them were some who had never had children, but with completely normal pelvic findings, and others who had several children, with the usual subsequent relaxation of pelvic structures. Some of the common departures from normal, such as fibroid tumors of the uterus, tipping of the uterus, and varicose veins in the area, were also present. Nonetheless the responses to sexual situations were substantially the same in all.

It is clear that for far too long a time the medical profession had a relatively fixed and static conception of the female sexual anatomy. Underlying this was the longstanding notion which ascribed passivity to the female and overlooked the dynamic changes and the interplay found in her cycle of sexual responsiveness and orgasm. The finding that the vagina congests and expands and that the cervix moves upwards at once raises a question regarding one of the standard contraceptive methods, the diaphragm. The question is simple: How does a diaphragm fitted to an unstimulated woman in a doctor's office behave in the same woman under the vastly different conditions of intercourse?

Fortunately the Washington University group did study this specific problem. Some of their findings doubtless explain why, as with virtually all other contraceptive methods, even the well-regarded diaphragm can occasionally fail. It was clearly demonstrated that the changes occurring in a sexually responding woman could make a diaphragm less snug in its positioning as a result of the rising upward of the uterus and cervix and the expansion of the vaginal area around the diaphragm. Differences were also seen, depending on whether or not the women had had previous deliveries. In those who had not, the firmness of support of the pelvic tissues acted to restrain the expansion associated with sexual excitement; hence the secure fit of the diaphragm—which is kept in position by pressure against the vaginal walls, which are in turn supported by muscles and other pelvic structures—was not significantly impaired. But it was found that the stretching of these structures with childbirth may to a variable extent impair the snugness of fit of the diaphragm. With vaginal expansion following sexual stimulation less hampered by surrounding supporting tissues, the net result is that in some women who have borne children a diaphragm which seems firmly in place may, under the influence of sexual excitation, tend to lose its seating. Dislodgement then becomes a possibility and, in some of the circumstances of the sex act, may actually occur.

The positions adopted for sexual intercourse and certain features of the sexual act itself are of importance in this connection. Dislodgement of the diaphragm is less likely to occur with the woman in the usual position—flat on her back—and rather more likely with such common variations as the woman-above or the knee-chest position. It has also been observed that the possibility of diaphragm dislodgement is increased in any of the sexual positions where there is repeated insertion of the penis. It is by no means uncommon during the thrusting pelvic movements of intercourse for the penis to come out briefly as a result of the pelvic pendular excursions. At the height of sexual excitement reinsertion is likely to be hurried and, because of the marked swelling at the vaginal entrance described above, is not always as easy as might be anticipated. Reentry of the penis under these circumstances, especially if repeated, may lead to dislodgement.

Observations were made after simulated or actual intercourse under various circumstances such as might well occur in any couple's married life. In a few such instances the diaphragm was found to be displaced to one side of the vagina, thus leaving the cervix completely unprotected. If care was used in reinserting the penis when the woman was in the knee-chest position, the possibility of dislodgement was diminished. In the woman-above position, particularly with women who had had one or more children, even with care the possibilities for dislodgement seemed to exist in at least four of the thirty observed cases.

All this is not by any means to be interpreted as implying that the diaphragm is a poor contraceptive technique. On the contrary, it has for many decades been the standard of reference in contraceptive efficiency. The fact that it can on occasion be dislodged no more alters its status than the fact that a condom can break belies *its* value as a contraceptive. However, these observations do go far to explain why the diaphragm is not a 100-per-cent perfect method and why even intelligent and cooperative users of it have occasionally run into an unplanned pregnancy. For these users, several conclusions can be drawn:

1. At the time that the diaphragm is fitted, as snug a fit as is comfortable should be sought for. What is a tight fit in the doctor's examining room may be definitely less so in the marital bedroom.

2. If you have had one or more children and use the diaphragm, check with your doctor as to whether fit is adequately snug to cover all possibilities.

3. In the usual position for sexual intercourse dislodgement is not to be anticipated when the initial fit is a good one. In other positions and when intercourse is vigorous, some care should be exerted. Withdrawal and reinsertion of the penis should be careful and unhurried, particularly in the female-above position.

Prudent couples given to experimentation with positions, especially if the woman has had one or more children, may even consider using a supplementary method with the diaphragm, such as the foam. This may be a worthwhile form of insurance.

Other observations recorded by Dr. Masters and his group are of importance to couples using such contraceptive methods as creams, foams, jellies, foaming tablets, and suppositories. There are several problems with the use of these agents. One is that uniform distribution is necessary so that wherever sperm are deposited they encounter a sufficient amount of the contraceptive preparation. A high concentration of a sperm-killing agent in one part of the vagina is of no value when semen is deposited elsewhere. In addition to reasonably uniform vaginal dispersion, it is necessary for some of the contraceptive to cling to the cervix and its opening since occasionally intercourse may provide an almost direct ejaculation of sperm over this area. Uniform distribution of these agents is enhanced by admixture with the vaginal lubricant fluid secreted during sexual stimulation, and also by the repeated penile thrusts. However, these two mechanisms cannot always be relied on to contribute to the needed contraceptive efficiency of some of these agents, such as the jellies. Thus if the man has too early an ejaculation, deposition of semen might occur with relatively few penile movements, and he could not be counted on to help produce dispersal of the contraceptive material. Other factors, perhaps of secondary importance, are leakage from the vagina due to lack of adherence or a "runny" quality of the material used. An excessive coating of the shaft of the penis is not likely to prove a major obstacle to the contraceptive goal but may still be regarded as somewhat objectionable in some instances.

When a number of these agents were studied under conditions of simulated or actual intercourse, some were found to be excellent, others failed to pass the test of actual practice. Thus a vaginal foaming tablet, even when adequate time had been allowed after its insertion, failed to disintegrate completely and coverage was inadequate. A vaginal suppository also recommended for contraceptive purposes suffered from similar defects. However, the better preparations, including two widely utilized ones, performed very adequately. The well-known Emko vaginal foam showed excellent distribution and coverage: in rigorous testing done with actual introduction of sperm, a rapidly lethal effect was demonstrated in different vaginal areas. Delfen Cream also showed good distribution and contraceptive efficiency. The foam had the further advantage of not causing any dripping, a complaint occasionally directed against the cream.

The jellies seemed inferior to the creams and foams in important respects. Only after a considerable amount of foreplay, with formation of lubricating fluid and helped along by continued penile distribution, was an adequate dispersion achieved during intercourse. Otherwise jellies inserted into one part of the vagina might be present in heavy concentration in one area with little or none present elsewhere. It was concluded that the contraceptive efficacy of some of the jellies, suppositories, and lesser creams is dependent on melting and dispersion by body heat and physical movements—sometimes too much so. When intercourse is short and ejaculation early, such preparations might not prove reliable for their purpose. It is therefore possible to rate the different products on a scale of reliability (p. 115).

Other explanations for failures derive from failure to follow directions carefully, rather than from difficulties inherent in the methods themselves. Thus a couple using a good cream or foam on retiring may safely have intercourse at the time, but may no longer have adequate protection if intercourse is repeated in the morning, when a second application of the medication may be necessary. Also with some women who have had babies it is felt that a double dose of the foam may be necessary for maximum protection. Finally it must be remembered that some of these agents leak out when a woman gets up to go to the bathroom or even when she stands up, coughs, or laughs.

It is a fortunate fact that the human species is relatively sterile rather than relatively fertile. Were this not so, failures of many standard or widely used contraceptive methods would be far more common. Unlike the situation in other species, the human female will accept the male just as readily during the sterile part of her cycle as at the time of ovulation. Because of the limited time of her fertility, much of the intercourse that human beings have could not possibly result in impregnation. Hence if on a rare occasion a diaphragm is dislodged or a contraceptive cream not adequately dispersed, or some other break in contraceptive technique occurs, nonetheless pregnancy will not result. Only a combination of certain circumstances leads to contraceptive failure in the form of pregnancy. The time of the month has to be right and a significant failure in the technique has to coincide with it. Sexual drives being what they are, combinations of events of this sort will sometimes occur. The observations recounted in this chapter help explain why it is that the contraceptive technique apparently efficacious in a test tube, and even effective in a given couple for months or for years can, in certain circumstances, fail. To illustrate, if such a technical failure coincides with the time of ovulation once in one hundred times, a couple who had been using a method successfully would run into an unexpected pregnancy once in eight years. Perhaps the moral is that though one can have very high levels of security by using several contraceptive methods, absolute security—like absolute beauty or absolute wealth—may not exist.

10.
What Method
To Choose?

In PRECEDING CHAPTERS WE have looked at some of the current acceptable methods of family planning. Perhaps there are two more that can be mentioned, neither of which is comparable to the various devices or medications discussed earlier. They are occasionally used by couples who are willing to run some risk or in circumstances where nothing else is available. One is a very old method indeed, since it is mentioned in the Old Testament as being used by Onan. It is technically known as *coitus interruptus* which is literally what it says— interrupted intercourse. Widely practiced in Europe as a method of family planning, it is reputed to be the chief reason for the fall in birth rate in France during the twentieth century. (France, a nominally Catholic country, frowns upon contraception; even birth control pills have to be smuggled in.) In coitus interruptus, known also as male withdrawal, the man withdraws when he feels the orgasm coming on. There is therefore no ejaculation of semen into the vagina and the orgasm occurs externally. This calls for a considerable degree of self-control on the part of the male, on whom full responsibility for avoiding impregnation will fall. There is no doubt that a few can practice this technique successfully year after year in their marital relationships without an unplanned pregnancy occurring. Overall it does not rank very high as a birth control technique. There are obvious drawbacks as well as hazards to coitus interruptus. A few major ones are the following:

1. Some sperm-containing fluid may leak out of the penis without the man's being aware. Though this does not always occur, it is a possibility that has to be reckoned with. Since it is known that a considerable number of sperm are necessary for fertilization of the egg to take place, there is some question as to how significant a little leakage containing relatively few sperm might be. But the chance is always there.

2. The need for interrupting intercourse to have an orgasm extravaginally puts a strain on the man. He has to be constantly evaluating himself as to whether an orgasm is coming. Also he may feel the need for withdrawing at about the time his partner is approaching an orgasm and she certainly will be most frustrated by withdrawal at this point.

3. The intimate satisfaction afforded by having intercourse with an ejaculation in the vagina is of course nullified by this technique. There is also the psychological disadvantage that the man's semen is looked upon as something to be dreaded or avoided, a source of risk and danger. These are far from the positive and satisfying feelings a couple should have in an intimate relationship.

4. Some genitourinary specialists feel that coitus interruptus may contribute to congestion of the prostate and to urinary difficulties in men. There is no clearcut evidence that this is so. However, it is entirely possible that intercourse

completed in the usual fashion may be better physically for both the partners.

Coitus interruptus is occasionally practiced by couples who are away from home and their contraceptive supplies, or are traveling in a country where birth control pills or contraceptive supplies are not available. It is a technique to be kept in mind for such unusual situations. Though certainly not to be commended as a long-term birth control method, it may serve in a pinch.

Another method which can be mentioned here for the sake of completeness but certainly not with the intimation that it can be a reliable contraceptive measure is douching immediately after intercourse. Sperm may be found ascending the cervical canal within ninety seconds after intercourse. Since their numbers doubtless steadily increase in the minutes following orgasm, the need for haste with a douche seems imperative. Probably the only reason why douching would work at all is through a drastic reduction in the number of sperm available for fertilization. Many hundreds of sperm in the vicinity of the egg seem to be necessary for one to fertilize it successfully. Douching may work—when it does work—by lowering the available number of sperm to too low a level for fertilization to occur.

The disadvantages of the douche are obvious and formidable. It requires that the woman get out of bed promptly, perhaps even before reaching her own orgasm. It means a major unwelcome interruption to relaxation, breaking the intimacy of the marital bed. When the need for douching arises on a chilly night, there is an added element of physical discomfort. Worst of all, douching is a poor substitute for all other methods, being far inferior even to coitus interruptus. In short, it is difficult, unreliable, and pleasure-destroying. There are various other inadequate contraceptive techniques which one may hear about. One is the insertion, beforehand, of a piece of sponge into which soap has been lathered, or which has been dipped in a strong salt or vinegar solution; and there are other similar primitive methods.

If we return to the standard methods, we may as well put all the cards on the table by stating in advance that there is no perfect contraceptive method. Such a perfect method would be one which would always work and never fail. It would not in any direct way be related to lovemaking in the sense of there being an interruption to don some device or other. It would not be complicated or cumbersome, nor require difficult manipulations. It would be effective under all circumstances of lovemaking, such as when intercourse is repeated at close intervals, or when different positions are used. It would be nonmessy and esthetically acceptable. It would not interfere with the completion of the normal sexual act nor require some special activities afterwards. Finally, it would be absolutely safe and have no untoward effects either locally or elsewhere in the body.

Needless to say no such agent, drug, or technique currently exists, nor does one seem imminent. We must compromise therefore and make do with what we have, finding the method which is of maximum acceptability and effectiveness in any given situation. The overall situation will vary at different phases of a married couple's life, so that a method recommended at one time may not necessarily be applicable at another. For example, it may be found after several deliveries that the diaphragm plus jelly, ordinarily a reliable and excellent technique, can no longer be used because a good fit can no longer be secured. Similarly, the birth control pills have not been approved for indefinite usage, but bear a time limit varying up to perhaps three to four years.

The Food and Drug Administration takes the position that a medication which has been observed in numerous women for say two to four years without any harmful side effects might conceivably not be as free of side effects with further years of usage. Although this is not likely to be the case and women have in fact been taking these pills for as long as seven years and even more, the fact is that a stated time limit has been set. Keep in mind that there is no regulatory body to warn you that your two or three years on a given pill are up and you may not take more. Indeed, many doctors have had no hesitation in permitting their patients to go on taking the drugs indefinitely.

Whatever the method selected, one should follow all of the details and precautions prescribed for its usage. These should be followed to the letter. Every episode of sexual intercourse may potentially be the one that results in pregnancy, and from the contraceptive viewpoint there should never be lapses in security. The hundreds of millions of sperm furnished by any act of intercourse are like miniature gladiators. They all have a "do it now or die" attitude. Whether or not you are interested in pregnancy, even if you are bitterly against the idea, sperm are at all times enthusiastically prone to turn in a peak performance in their race towards the egg cell. Hence precautions must be used each and every time. However elementary this sounds, the fact is that many contraceptive failures turn out to be due to a "Russian roulette" attitude which may crop up on a particular occasion. A couple who have been faithfully following prescribed measures decides just this once to take a chance. When passions are high, judgment as to the possibility of pregnancy may be dulled. Indeed, some couples seem to throw themselves on the mercy of fate. Having successfully staved off pregnancy by using contraceptives for, say, a year, they may decide on a specific night to throw caution to the wind and run that little bit of risk just once. Now some may successfully snap their fingers at fate many times, but others find they cannot do so even once.

A distinction is sometimes drawn between the theoretical effectiveness of a contraceptive method and its effectiveness in actual use. A method which may be quite a good one if a sequence of four different steps is followed may have its value impaired if at the final stage carelessness creeps in—as, for example, if a woman using a diaphragm fails to check to be sure that the cervix is covered by it. Some couples using a specific contraceptive method will regularly do better than others, and the differences are due to motivation and care in following instructions rather than drawbacks in the method itself. Are you forgetful? You may fail to take the pill every 24 hours. If you are honest and realistic about yourself, your choice of a contraceptive method may be a better informed one, and over the long run, serve you better. If you have a tendency to be impatient with all details, perhaps you should seek out the simplest of the reliable methods, such as an intrauterine device.

Here are some other points to be kept in mind regarding the choice of contraceptive methods:

1. A married couple must plan together. No aspect of marriage is more vital, none carries more long-term implications and responsibilities than the planning with respect to the possibility of pregnancy. There must be a meeting of minds regarding such important decisions as when to have the baby, how many to have, how they should be spaced. These aspects of marriage and reproduction cannot be settled unilaterally. The "let him worry about it" attitude, or perhaps more commonly the "let her worry about it" male viewpoint may breed great discontent as well as babies. A woman who finds herself repeatedly becoming pregnant because her husband is a careless user of the condom may well come to have deep feelings of anger and resentment over this carelessness and indifference. Serious marital strife and frigidity may build up in the wife if she feels that an unwanted pregnancy is the price she may be asked to pay each time she has intercourse. Sometimes the situation may be reversed. A woman with strong maternal urges, anxious to have more babies than is her husband, may become careless or forgetful with her diaphragm. Again, unless the basic issue is resolved and a harmony of views attained, hostility or negativism in the male may result. Let

there be spontaneity in your sex life and planning in your reproductive life.

2. Each partner may, at one time or another, have to be willing to assume responsibility. Let us assume that a woman has been using the pill for several years, has then had a planned pregnancy. If she wishes to nurse the baby— and there is much to be said for this—she should not resume the pill. Nor can she use a diaphragm and jelly, at least not too soon after the birth of the baby. It may then fall upon the husband to use a technique such as the condom as an interim method. Similarly, the condom is often a useful method to be used on the honeymoon if the woman has not been started on pills, and has not learned the use of a diaphragm or other methods.

3. The method used must be physically and esthetically acceptable to both parties. If a tablet, cream, or jelly produces irritation either to the man or the woman, there is no need for putting up with it. A change to another manufacturer's brand or an alternative method should be tried.

4. A choice regarding effectiveness should be made. This may be conditioned by various factors and is perhaps best discussed with the doctor. One important factor he may consider is the degree of sexual drive and the frequency of sexual intercourse. With a young couple having intercourse frequently, the chances of impregnation are certainly higher than with an older couple having intercourse but a few times a month. For an older couple, the daily taking of the pill may seem overly cautious and, if the woman has had a clot or vein problem, may be inadvisable. A foam, or a contraceptive cream or a condom may be a reasonably good answer and in the over-all sense simpler than the pill.

5. Does pregnancy present a special hazard either physically or psychologically? To a woman in an emotionally disturbed frame of mind, the finding that she has become pregnant may have a devastating impact. A woman who has had an operation for certain breast tumors should by

all means be protected against pregnancy. Other medical conditions, such as rheumatic heart disease, kidney disease, severe degrees of high blood pressure, or perhaps a history of several caesarean sections, might all be imperative reasons for using the most effective technique for preventing pregnancy.

With many contraceptive methods, a great deal of accumulated experience allows one to make a judgment as to the degrees of effectiveness of the different approaches. They are derived from observations at various birth control clinics in different parts of the country where the records of a large number of women have been followed after instruction in the use of one or another method. It may well be that your experience with a specific method may be better than the figures below indicate. This is due to the fact that an intelligent, well-motivated couple using care in following details may have a better success rate than a less motivated couple. For example, it has been shown that the same couple, as they continue to use the same method, have fewer failures after they have had a number of children. This follows from the fact that at this point in their life, motivation against having more babies will favorably affect use of the particular technique.

But when due allowance is made for motivation and attention to detail, there are intrinsic differences in the different methods. A standard way of expressing the effectiveness is in terms of the number of pregnancies to be observed in a group of 100 women using a particular method for a year. In a normally fertile group of 100 women, one would expect about 80 pregnancies in the course of a year. Maximum effectiveness for a contraceptive method, of course, would be zero, a figure that seems to be attainable only by use of the pill. Even the rare failures reported by some pill users seem to be due to failure to take the pill each day according to the directions.

Here then for your guidance is what the different contraceptive methods can be expected to do, arranged in decreasing order of effectiveness:

	METHOD	PREGNANCY RATE/YEAR PER 100 WOMEN
Most Effective	{ Pill	1.2
	{ Intrauterine device	2.4
Reasonably Effective	{ Condom	12
	{ Diaphragm	14
	{ Foam	14
Less Reliable	{ Withdrawal	18
	{ Jelly alone	20
	{ Rhythm	24
Unreliable	Douche	31

As can be seen, this table in a sense records failures only, not successes. Thus the pill, which most observers feel should be 100 per cent effective, is somewhat less so with at least certain groups of women, a few of whom apparently forget to take it daily. Nonetheless it does rank as number one on all lists. The intrauterine device (IUCD) has a somewhat higher failure rate, primarily because of unnoted expulsion. The rate reported here is for the first year of use, when most of the expulsions occur. In the second year of use the failure rate drops to perhaps half that reported for the initial year, and at that point the IUCD is practically, though not quite, the equal of the pill in effectiveness.

There are several further conclusions that can be drawn from this. There is no method which guarantees against an unplanned pregnancy, even though with reasonable care and with a reasonably good method unplanned pregnancy should not be anticipated. If the marital situation calls for maximum protection, the pill would be the method of first choice; but if for any medical reason the pill cannot be taken, consider the advantages of combining more than one method. Dr. Mary Calderone has described such a combined method whose effectiveness should approach that offered by the pill. It calls for keeping track of the fertile period as described in the chapter following; a foam plus the condom should be used during the fertile week or until the rise in body temperature indicates that ovulation did take place; three days after this rise, or at times other than the fertile week, the foam alone can be used.

But whatever method you choose, be sure to use it faithfully and in accordance with instructions.

The Reduction of Fertility: *OTHER APPROACHES*

11.
Safe Period and Rhythm Method

U<small>P UNTIL A FEW</small> decades ago, it was generally thought that women could ovulate at almost any time in the cycle. A few authorities leaned to the idea that ovulation might occur around the time of menstruation. It was also thought that sperm might retain their vitality in the female reproductive tract for very long periods. Finally there was even a theory that intense sexual stimulation and intercourse might provoke ovulation in a woman, a biologic situation known to occur in the rabbit where ovulation regularly occurs about 10 to 12 hours after mating. The notion that a woman could become pregnant only during a limited period in the entire menstrual month, and that intercourse without precautions at all other times could not possibly result in pregnancy, is a relatively recent idea. It was first generally propounded around 1930.

However, once the scientific information reviewed in the preceding chapters had been accumulated, there emerged the concept of fertile and infertile phases in a woman's menstrual month. The reasoning behind this concept can be readily followed. The basic points to keep in mind are the following:

1. The egg is released from the ovary at around the middle of the cycle. Many observations made in many different ways indicate that in a typical 28-day cycle most of the ovulations occur on Days 11, 12, 13, 14, and 15 of the cycle, counting the first day of menstruation as Day 1. Ovulation before or after these days can occur but is much less frequent.

2. There is only one single episode of ovulation in a menstrual cycle. Once an egg has been released, whether or not it is fertilized, no further eggs will be made in that cycle.

3. The egg cell is a large but delicate and fragile cell. To survive, it must be fertilized by a sperm within 24 hours, perhaps even less. Forty-eight hours after its release, the unfertilized egg shows unmistakable signs of degeneration. Numerous experiments have shown that after 12 to 24 hours the egg is truly "stale." Such a stale egg does not develop properly even if sperm are made available to it.

4. Probably intercourse cannot result in pregnancy 24 hours after ovulation, and certainly it cannot so result 48 hours after ovulation or at any time later during the rest of the cycle. The entire latter phase of the menstrual cycle would therefore be "safe."

5. What is the situation if sperm are present as a result of intercourse prior to ovulation? Once in the female reproductive tract, sperm retain their fertilizing ability for probably no more than three days. Sperm older than this simply disintegrate, after passing through a phase in which, though still motile, they cannot fertilize the egg.

6. Hence there is only a limited period, measured in

a time span of a few days, during which a woman can become pregnant. At all other times she cannot conceive no matter how frequent intercourse may be. This span extends from some three days before the time of ovulation to no more than a day or so past it. A liberal estimate, taking into account all the known facts, would make the period of fertility in any given menstrual cycle no more than four days, and more likely it is somewhat less. The four-day period (more or less) during which intercourse could result in pregnancy is known as the fertile period. All the other days prior to and subsequent to this four-day period, days on which impregnation is not possible, are therefore referred to as the safe period. Family planning based on utilization of a knowledge of safe and fertile periods is known as the rhythm method.

Married couples who use the rhythm method for control of pregnancy avoid the necessity for taking pills, using mechanical devices, foams, jellies, and the like. They must, however, keep track of the menstrual cycle and practice abstention from intercourse during the fertile period. Particular interest has extended to the rhythm method of birth control because so far it is the only method of family planning sanctioned by the Roman Catholic Church. Many gadgets, such as slide rules, specially prepared calendars, and even a special clock have been brought forth to aid women in calculating the safe and unsafe phases of their menstrual cycles. However, the method is not applicable to all couples; it has some drawbacks both in theory and practice; and one should understand the simple ideas and calculations behind the rhythm method rather than blindly rely on any gadget. Let us therefore take a close look at who can practice the rhythm method, and how it should be practiced.

Who Can Practice Rhythm?

The rhythm method can be used by women only if they have reasonably regular menstrual cycles. A woman whose cycle is 23 days one month, 33 days the next month, and 28 days the succeeding month, is already too irregular to use this method successfully—even though her cycles may all add up to a 28-day average. It has been learned from many sad experiences that women tend to think they are more regular than in fact they are. Their recollections tend to cluster around the 28-day cycles and omit shorter or longer ones. Thus a woman who in the course of a year has ten 28-day cycles, plus one short cycle of 24 days and one long cycle of 32 days, may honestly think she is quite regular. From the point of view of safe cycle calculation, however, she is far from being as regular as is desirable. *The closer the clustering of the menstrual cycles, the better for the rhythm method.* A woman whose periods regularly recur at 27 or 28 or 29 days is a far better candidate for using rhythm than the woman ten of whose cycles are 28 days "on the button" but who has also had one much longer and one much shorter cycle.

Women early and also late in their menstrual lifetime— that is very young women and women approaching the menopause—have more irregularities in cycle length than the sexually mature woman in her early twenties and thirties. Thus, in some young women, irregularity may be succeeded by regularity to be followed again by irregularity. Only when it has been established that there is reasonable regularity is the rhythm method applicable. To decide this, it is best not to rely on memory. In fact, proponents of the rhythm method generally require that a year's cycles be charted to ascertain the existence of reasonable regularity and to gather the necessary facts for calculating the safe cycle. What above all else is necessary for safe application of this method is *regularity*.

How to Use the Safe Period

Let us suppose that you are one of the few women who really menstruate regularly every 28 days. It is probable that you ovulate around the fourteenth day of the cycle, counting the first day of menstruation as Day 1 of the cycle. However, it is also possible that you could ovulate on Day 13 or even Day 12 of the cycle. Or you may ovulate on Day 15 and also quite conceivably on Day 16 of the cycle. It is not possible to tell with the onset of a menstrual period and the beginning of a new cycle whether you are going to ovulate a little earlier or a little later than average *in that particular cycle.* Therefore in calculating your safe and unsafe periods you would have to take into account *a range* of several days on each of which ovulation might occur— perhaps as early as Days 10 or 11, perhaps as late as Days 15 or 16.

Since we have to allow several days for sperm survival, the fertility situation takes form somewhat as follows: If you had intercourse on Day 10 of the cycle and ovulated on Day 12, pregnancy might result. Indeed, granted the sperm can fertilize an egg for 72 hours, then conceivably intercourse on Day 9 of the cycle with ovulation three days later—Day 12—might also result in pregnancy. Hence Day 9 of the cycle could certainly represent the beginning of the fertile period. When would this fertile period end? Probably about 24 hours after ovulation, whenever that occurs. Suppose ovulation occurred on Day 15 of the cycle. Allowing for 24 hours during which the egg could be fertilized, intercourse on Day 16 of the cycle could, with a late ovulation, also result in pregnancy. So, even with a woman who is quite regular—"28 days"—our calculations lead us to the potential of an entire fertile week. This week would extend from Day 9 through Day 16 of the menstrual cycle. Intercourse on any day during that fertile week might *conceivably* result in pregnancy. The converse should also be true: Intercourse prior to Day 9 or after Day 16 of such a cycle would *not* result in pregnancy.

Suppose now that occasional cycles are longer, say 30 or 31 days. Do we have to change these calculations? The answer is yes. In the 30-day cycle, ovulation might occur on Day 17 of the cycle, and in such a cycle it would not be safe to have intercourse until the eighteenth day—so that now the range of the fertile period has to be extended. It is just these occasional long or short cycles that make for difficulties and increase the duration of sexual abstinence.

About 80 per cent of all women have reasonably regular menstrual cycles for purposes of rhythm calculations. These women are not necessarily regular in a clocklike manner but are sufficiently regular for this method. They fall into the group whose cycles are 28 days plus or minus 3. That is, the menstrual cycles extend over a range of some 25 to 31 days, with an average of 28 days, perhaps with most of the cycles 28 days. Since one cannot know at the beginning of any given menstrual cycle whether it will be a short one of 25 days or a long one of 31 days, the calculations will necessarily have to be adjusted to this range of possibilities. There are at least two differing methods by which to calculate the safe and unsafe parts of the cycle. Though the general ideas held by different authorities are similar, the limits set up for the fertile period will vary a day or two at either end, depending on which method of calculation one chooses to follow. The two physicians who have written extensively on this problem are the Japanese doctor, Ogino, and the German gynecologist, Knaus. Their description of the fertile period is sometimes referred to as the Ogino-Knaus theory. Each has independently shown that if intercourse is avoided during the fertile period (as calculated by his own method) the expected number of pregnancies goes down drastically. However, Ogino's method gives a somewhat longer fertile period than Knaus's method, so some authorities feel that the Ogino method (which we shall adhere to) is the safest.

An easy and satisfactory way of calculating the fertile period is the following:

1. One should have a record of the menstrual periods for the preceding year, so as to be able to calculate the range of variability. In a pinch, six months of records will do, but keep track of your subsequent cycles. From these data you can readily determine the number of days in the shortest as well as the longest cycle. If you have no record of previous cycles but believe you have been reasonably regular, for calculation's sake adopt a range of from 25 to 31 days—and start charting your cycles.

2. Subtract 18 from the shortest cycle. Subtract 10 from the longest cycle. The two numbers thus arrived at represent the outer limits of the fertile period.

As an example, suppose that the preceding year's menstrual cycles have varied from 25 to 31 days in length. Subtracting 18 from the shortest cycle gives us the number 7 (25 minus 18 equals 7). Subtracting 10 from the longest cycles gives us 21 (31 minus 10 equals 21). The total range of the fertile period would then be from Day 7 to Day 21 Intercourse before Day 7 or after Day 21 should not result in pregnancy.

It follows, of course, that the more regular the menstrual cycles, the narrower the limits of the fertile period. Suppose, as an example, that all cycles for the preceding year have been either 27, 28, or 29 days. Then the fertile period would extend from Days 9 to 19. In such a woman the period of abstinence for purposes of the rhythm method would be the ten days from Day 9 to 19 rather than the fourteen days from Day 7 to 21 in the more variable case cited above.

In the case of the absolutely regular woman with a recurrent 28-day cycle, the fertile period would extend from Day 10 to Day 18. Intercourse before Day 10 or after Day 18 would fall into the infertile or safe period of the cycle.

Always provided your cycle length is not too irregular to have the rhythm method apply, you can easily determine your fertile period from following Table I. No other calculator is necessary; all you need is a calendar to facilitate figuring out the days in the month involved. Remember always that the first day of menstruation is Day 1 of the cycle. If your cycle lengths have been 27 to 29 days, your fertile period is from Day 9 through Day 19. Unless you alter your menstrual pattern so that these cycle lengths change, you need not recalculate your fertile period. All you have to keep in mind is that Days 9 to 19 are applicable to each cycle. The calculations are then quite simple for any given calendar month. Thus, if you had a menstrual period beginning March 1, your fertile period would be March 9 to March 19. If your next menstrual period occurred on March 28 that would be Day 1 of the next menstrual cycle. Your fertile period would then be April 5 to the 15th.

With this table, you should have no difficulty in calculating your fertile period. Simply read down it until you find the range of days corresponding to your different menstrual cycles. On the same calendar on which you keep track of your menstrual periods, you can readily check off the days of your fertility. So long as your menstrual periods continue to fall within a reasonably regular range, you can use this kind of table.

There is no doubt that for many women the rhythm method works out well as a technique for controlling pregnancy. This is particularly the case when the cycles are quite regular and when the couple faithfully adheres to the schedule. An example of the successful application of the rhythm method adapted from an actual record illustrates this. Here a recently married woman utilized rhythm to avoid pregnancy for eight months. then promptly became pregnant on having intercourse during her fertile period. She had always been quite regular, with cycles varying from 27 to 29 days. Hence her fertile period extends from Day 9 to Day 19.

TABLE I. The Fertile Period

IF YOUR SHORTEST CYCLE IS

22 days, the fertile period begins on day							4
23 "	"	"	"	"	"	"	5
24 "	"	"	"	"	"	"	6
25 "	"	"	"	"	"	"	7
26 "	"	"	"	"	"	"	8
27 "	"	"	"	"	"	"	9
28 "	"	"	"	"	"	"	10
29 "	"	"	"	"	"	"	11
30 "	"	"	"	"	"	"	12
31 "	"	"	"	"	"	"	13
32 "	"	"	"	"	"	"	14
33 "	"	"	"	"	"	"	15
34 "	"	"	"	"	"	"	16

IF YOUR LONGEST CYCLE IS

22 days, the fertile period extends through day							12
23 "	"	"	"	"	"	"	13
24 "	"	"	"	"	"	"	14
25 "	"	"	"	"	"	"	15
26 "	"	"	"	"	"	"	16
27 "	"	"	"	"	"	"	17
28 "	"	"	"	"	"	"	18
29 "	"	"	"	"	"	"	19
30 "	"	"	"	"	"	"	20
31 "	"	"	"	"	"	"	21
32 "	"	"	"	"	"	"	22
33 "	"	"	"	"	"	"	23
34 "	"	"	"	"	"	"	24

TABLE II. Rhythm Method and Control of Conception

CYCLE	FERTILE PERIOD	Days and markers
MARCH 3-29	(11-21)	3 4 5 6 7 8 9 10 | 11 12 13 14 15 16 17 18 19 20 21 | 22 23 24 25 26 27 28 29
		M M M M M I I | F F F F F F F F F F F | I I I I
MAR. 30-APR. 26	(7-17)	30 31 1 2 3 4 5 6 | 7 8 9 10 11 12 13 14 15 16 17 | 18 19 20 21 22 23 24 25 26
		M M M M M I I I | F F F F F F F F F F F | I I I I I
APR. 27-MAY 24	(5-15)	27 28 29 30 1 2 3 4 | 5 6 7 8 9 10 11 12 13 14 15 | 16 17 18 19 20 21 22 23 24
		M M M M M I I | F F F F F F F F F F F | I I I I I I I
MAY 25-JUN. 21	(2-12)	25 26 27 28 29 30 31 1 | 2 3 4 5 6 7 8 9 10 11 12 | 13 14 15 16 17 18 19 20 21
		M M M M M I I | F F F F F F F F F F F | I I I I I
JUN. 22-JUL. 18	(30-10)	22 23 24 25 26 27 28 29 | 30 1 2 3 4 5 6 7 8 9 10 | 11 12 13 14 15 16 17 18
		M M M M M I I | F F F F F F F F F F F | I I I
JUL. 19-AUG. 16	(27-6)	19 20 21 22 23 24 25 26 | 27 28 29 30 31 1 2 3 4 5 6 | 7 8 9 10 11 12 13 14 15
		M M M M M I I | F F F F F F F F F F F | I I I I I
AUG. 17-SEP. 13	(25-5)	17 18 19 20 21 22 23 24 | 25 26 27 28 29 30 1 2 3 4 5 | 6 7 8 9 10 11 12 13
		M M M M M I I | F F F F F F F F F F F | I I I I
SEP. 14-OCT. 10	(22-2)	14 15 16 17 18 19 20 21 | 22 23 24 25 26 27 28 29 30 1 2 | 3 4 5 6 7 8 9 10
		M M M M M I I | F F F F F F F F F F F | I I I I
OCT. 11-	(19-PREGNANCY)	11 12 13 14 15 16 17 18 19 20 21 22 23 24 25 26 27 28 29 30 31 1 2 3 4 5 6
		M M M M M M I I I I I I I I I . . . PREGNAN*

M – MENSTRUATION   I – INTERCOURSE   F – FERTILE

* 9 month record of exposure to conception by one patient using the rhythm method.

Why the Rhythm Method Might Fail

Actual experience over a period of many years indicates that for many women who menstruate regularly the rhythm method can be used successfully as an approach to preventing pregnancy. But as a birth control method applied to large groups of women, the rhythm method is definitely less successful than the use of mechanical devices, such as the diaphragm or condom, and far inferior to the pill. Some of the simplified versions of the rhythm method make it all sound so very simple that couples are honestly surprised to encounter an unplanned pregnancy. Some of the charts, rulers, fertility clocks, or other devices for calculating the safe period have a spurious air of certainty about them. What could possibly go wrong with a calculating device which gives the safe period in black, the fertile period in red?

The answer is that sometimes a calculator designed to predict a machine's performance may be more accurate than the machine itself. The general idea behind safe cycle calculations is certainly correct: it simply holds that the egg is released about two weeks before the ensuing menstrual period. Possibly in some instances ovulation may be a bit earlier or later, say 15 or 16 days—or 11 or 12 days—before the next menstrual period, rather than the precise 14 days argued for by some rhythm adherents. But when will the next menstrual period be? No one can be sure at the beginning of one cycle when the next menstrual period will occur. Looking over the record of the preceding cycles covering a year or even longer enables one to make a prediction—but this is a guess based on experience, not a prophecy that contains built-in certainty.

The way in which variability of menstrual cycles may trip up adherents to the rhythm method can be illustrated as follows:

1. *A long cycle*—Let us assume that all previous cycles

have been approximately 28 days, so that the fertile period extended from Day 10 to Day 18. Suppose now for one or another unknown reason a menstrual cycle were suddenly to occur in which ovulation was delayed until, for example, around Day 19, as may very well happen in a 33-day cycle. On the basis of their previous experiences with 28-day cycles, a couple would assume that the nineteenth day of the new cycle was the beginning of the safe period, whereas in fact it would be the day of ovulation. Such a prolongation of cycle length could thus result in pregnancy.

2. *A short cycle*—Now let us suppose that, again for an unknown reason, the reproductive clock was speeded up and the previous 28-day woman just this once becomes a 23-day one. In such a cycle ovulation could occur on Day 9, previously regarded as a safe day, and so intercourse on that day might result in pregnancy. Of course, such a short or long cycle may never occur, or it may perhaps occur once in several years. But no one can know with certainty that it will not occur in the near, not the distant future.

The fact is that very infrequently with some women, perhaps more frequently with others, a cycle of shorter or longer length does occur. There is good evidence for believing that the interval between the time of ovulation and the time of the next menstruation is the least variable part of any variable cycle. It is approximately a 14-day interval. Hence in longer cycles ovulation tends to occur later, and in shorter cycles earlier, than is usually the case. *If such early or late ovulations transcend the previous limits of the safe period, intercourse on "safe" days may result in pregnancy.* Hence the rhythm method is a method that works successfully only for women who are fairly regular in their menstrual cycles and whose cycles stay regular. It simply will not work for women whose cycles are irregular. Even with women who are moderately irregular the number of days that have to be allotted to the possible fertile period may be so numerous as to make the number of safe days simply too few. For example, in a woman whose cycles vary from 23 to 33 days, the calculated fertile period will range from Day 5 to Day 23. This calls for an 18-day period of abstinence which, perhaps superimposed on the days of menstruation, means prolonged sexual abstinence indeed.

This brings us to another reason why the rhythm method may fail, which is that it imposes a degree of discipline and self-restraint not all couples can always maintain. When both partners have well-developed sex drives, a regime that calls for even a ten-day period of abstinence may be trying. It may be tempting to cut a corner, say by having intercourse on the last day of the fertile period (a day before the safe period begins), on the assumption that it is "probably safe." Though one may be able to clip a day or so off each end of the fertile period (by following the method of Knaus as against that of Ogino) this leads rhythm adherents into a game of taking chances.

The rhythm method will considerably reduce the chances of pregnancy in any group of women. But it may not reduce the probability of pregnancy sufficiently for a specific woman. To a woman with very regular cycles who uses the rhythm method with the hope of spacing pregnancies and to whom an unexpected pregnancy would not be a disaster, the method may be quite acceptable. This could well be the situation with many Catholic couples who accept this method of family planning as the only one allowed them. For others, particularly if there are important reasons for not getting pregnant, the rhythm method may not provide sufficient assurance.

There are ways in which the applicability of the rhythm method may be reliably increased. Combining rhythm with the taking of basal body temperatures (BBT) yields a combination of greater value. Consider, for example, the woman whose fertile period extends from Day 10 to Day 18 of her cycle. If the BBT shows a marked drop on Day 12, an unequivocal rise on Day 13, with a maintenance of the rise on the succeeding days, this woman might accurately conclude that she ovulated on Day 12. In such an instance, the resumption of sexual relations on Day 16—several days ahead of the schedule called for by safe period calculations —is reasonably safe. Some couples utilize the facts behind the rhythm theory as a guide to increased precautions but do not rely on the rhythm theory alone. For example, a couple that uses the foam—a contraceptive method of moderate though not absolute efficiency—can further decrease the small possibility of pregnancy if the man additionally uses a condom during the fertile period of the cycle. Thus, for the regular woman with the 28-day cycle, foam plus condom would be used from Days 8 to 18, the foam alone on other days.

Because the rhythm method is a technique so important and widely used, and because in its original form its reliability has been admittedly quite inferior to pills and mechanical devices, a good deal of thoughtful attention has gone into modifying or improving it. And indeed it has been found that, if combined with careful temperature taking, its reliability does improve in several respects.

1. When a well-defined rise in basal body temperature is observed, so that ovulation is probable, and this is validated by the temperature remaining up for at least three days, we may say that the safe portion of the cycle has begun. Some of the calendar days which might otherwise be regarded as unsafe can thus become safe, and the period of sexual abstinence is shortened.

2. The problem area seems to be the time directly prior to ovulation. In fact, many of the unplanned pregnancies that do occur in adherents to the rhythm method are believed to be due to unexpected, irregular, early ovulation (at a time which the woman has every reason to consider safe), perhaps coinciding with a particularly favorable survival time for sperm. Thus intercourse on Days 7 or 8 of the cycle, with ovulation occurring on Day 9 or 10—which

may be several days earlier than in previous cycles—results in pregnancy.

Since it is easier to tell when ovulation occurs *in retrospect* than *in prospect,* couples that depend on the rhythm method may find it more reliable if they become aware of the following modifications, arrived at during the Second International Symposium on Rhythm in December, 1965. The modifications are as follows:

1. The only absolutely safe part of the cycle is that *following* ovulation.

2. All the days after the end of active menstrual bleeding should be regarded as relatively unsafe, becoming more so as the time of ovulation approaches.

3. It is therefore safest to abstain from sexual relations from the time active bleeding ends until 72 hours after the rise in basal body temperature has occurred. A significant temperature shift is considered one which is at least 0.4° F. above the previous baseline and which is maintained for at least three days. The baseline is the average of the five days preceding the temperature shift.

4. These modifications, based on temperature change and the timing of ovulation, are considered superior to all other calculation methods in which the calendar alone was used as a guide.

There is one further word of caution regarding use of the rhythm method. Resumption of normal menstrual cycles may be somewhat erratic during the months immediately after labor and delivery. Nursing also often delays the onset of menstrual cycles. However, continuation of breast feeding cannot be relied on as a contraceptive method, especially as the months after the delivery go by. In fact, some women ovulate and become pregnant while nursing a baby even before a first menstrual period has resumed. In the uncertain circumstances following childbirth it may not be possible to apply the rhythm method, and other techniques may have to be used.

12.
Sterilization

$\mathbf{A}$s we have seen, birth control measures consist of a wide variety of methods for diminishing or doing away with the possibility of pregnancy—whether by means of pills, use of the rhythm technique, mechanical barriers, or sperm-killing agents. All these methods are essentially reversible solutions to the problem of fertility and consequent pregnancy.

From time to time fears have been expressed as to the use of one or another method. "If I stop using it," women want to know, "can I get pregnant if I want to?" The same question has been raised regarding almost every contraceptive method known, most recently with the intrauterine contraceptive device and with the birth control pills. The answer in all instances is that the ability to become pregnant is promptly restored once the method is abandoned—in fact, a considerable number of women become pregnant a month or two after the intrauterine device is removed or the pills stopped. Indeed, so far as the pill is concerned, some of the early investigations suggested apparently enhanced fertility in the months immediately following discontinuance of the pill.

Sterilization, however, stands in sharp contrast to all other methods. Usually a surgical procedure, it renders the person on whom it is performed permanently incapable of having offspring. This is applicable to either sex. The approach and the reasoning underlying sterilization are simple to understand. In essence the method relies on the surgical interruption of the pathways along which the sex cells must travel.

In the case of the woman, at the time of fertility the egg, shortly after being released from the ovary, enters the opening of the tube. Passage of the egg down the tube to the uterus is known to take three days. It is also well established that the egg is most frequently fertilized by the sperm in the portion of the tube adjacent to the ovary. In fact, fertilization of the egg by the sperm probably must occur within twelve to twenty-four hours after the egg is released. Perhaps most often the male sperm cells have already made their way up into the ovarian end of the tube and are waiting there to welcome any newly arrived egg.

Permanent sterilization of the female can be easily accomplished by a procedure known as tubal ligation. The simple surgical method for doing this is to tie each tube tightly in two places fairly close together, generally at about the middle of the tube, then cut it between the ties, much in the same way as one cuts the umbilical cord. Once cut, the tube ceases to be a continuous channel; in addition, the two cut ends are sealed off by the ties. This particular method was evolved because experience showed that cutting alone did not always yield the desired result: In some instances the two ends could and did grow together.

With the tube cut and tied in this manner, a permanent form of sterility follows. The sperm cells may, as before,

TUBAL LIGATION AND CONTRACEPTION

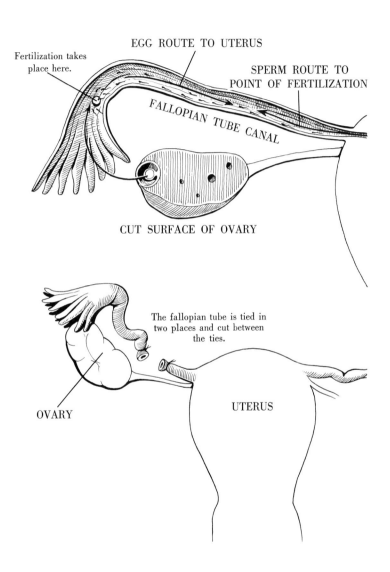

EGG ROUTE TO UTERUS

Fertilization takes place here.

SPERM ROUTE TO POINT OF FERTILIZATION

FALLOPIAN TUBE CANAL

CUT SURFACE OF OVARY

The fallopian tube is tied in two places and cut between the ties.

OVARY

UTERUS

FIGURE 20

make their way up from the vagina through the uterus and into the tubes, but their progress is arrested when they encounter the cut, tied-off sections. After a few days the sperm simply degenerate and dissolve. A similar sequence of events occurs on the other side of the tied-off tube, this time involving the egg. The egg will make its way down the tube to the point of ligation, where no sperm can be encountered, and soon it too fragments and disappears. Since the sperm and the egg never meet, there can be no possibility of pregnancy.

Tubal ligation as a contraceptive measure has much to recommend it as compared to all the other methods described elsewhere in this book. Among its advantages are the following:

1. There is no alteration in normal glandular activity. In contrast to the situation created when the pill is taken, the ovary is unaffected: The usual monthly changes continue to occur in the ovary and the uterus, and there is no interference with hormone production or the action of the master gland, the pituitary. Whatever advantages there are in a woman being under the influence of her own hormones rather than those supplied by the manufacturer in pill form, certainly these advantages go along with the tubal ligation approach, as with the barrier and other methods.

2. Similarly, there is no interference with any other aspect of sexual performance. Sexual interest and capacity are not affected, nor is any other aspect of the sexual act impaired.

3. Since the method is permanent, absolute freedom from pregnancy is assured. It is no longer necessary for a woman to remember first to take pills and then to stop them, to check for the presence of a device, or to go through nightly insertion rituals with devices like the diaphragm. Also, she cannot run out of protection in a foreign country where pills or devices are unobtainable, and there is never a "forgetting" problem.

4. Finally, the method is 100 per cent effective. In this respect it is superior even to the vanishingly small pregnancy rate found among women using the pills, and certainly well ahead of the contraceptive effectiveness of the IUCD.

Though probably some thousands of tubal ligations are performed each year, its effectiveness and permanence when compared to other contraceptive methods would lead one to anticipate a far more widespread use of this method. With so much to be said for it, why isn't it more popular? Two major hurdles seem to stand in the way.

1. An abdominal operation is necessary to gain access to the tubes. This, of course, requires anesthesia; and there is the further drawback of at least a short stay in the hospital. In practice, tubal ligation is perhaps most often performed when a woman is already in the hospital for the birth of a baby. The operation is also technically simpler at this time. All the reproductive structures including the tubes are enlarged because of pregnancy, and the tubes are readily accessible through a small incision, and easily tied off. In fact, a tubal ligation performed under such conditions does not even add to the length of time a woman would spend in the hospital. Also, at this time the operation may be done with use of only a local anesthetic, thus bypassing the need for general anesthesia.

2. Irreversibility. *Tubal ligation is a permanent method of producing sterility.* A woman committed to taking the pill or using a diaphragm may change her mind and decide to have another baby, in which case all she has to do is simply to discontinue whatever contraceptive method she has been using. Not so with tubal ligation. Though it is occasionally possible to restore continuity to a ligated tube by a delicate surgical procedure, the probability of doing this successfully is rather low.

It is the difficulty of foreseeing the future that often leads to hesitation in the use of tubal ligation. Even though a woman may be entirely certain that she wants no more children, permanently cutting off her capacity to reproduce cannot always be done with the assurance that the decision may not be regretted some day. Consider for example the following instance: After five difficult pregnancies and four difficult deliveries Mrs. H. G. decided at the age of 29 that her family was large enough. She had a tubal ligation three days after the delivery of her fourth child. Some months later her husband died in a car accident, and after a few years she remarried. This was the first marriage for her second husband who was anxious to have children of his own. An attempt to restore continuity to the tubes failed. No children resulted from this second marriage, to the husband's great disappointment.

Admittedly cases of this sort are rare, but every doctor in his career has seen a few such unusual situations. The following is another example: Mrs. A. G., after three successful caesarean deliveries, feeling that her family was large enough and that she wanted freedom from fear of further pregnancy, requested a tubal ligation. Two years later one of her children died from an accidental overdose of aspirin. A further tragedy occurred in the following year, when a second child contracted encephalitis and was left with permanent brain damage. At this point Mrs. A. G. wanted to reverse her decision to have no more pregnancies, and a surgical attempt was made to rejoin the tubes. It was not successful.

Cases of this sort do not negate the fundamental advantages of tubal ligation, any more than the existence of automobile accidents prevents one from stepping into his automobile. But experiences of this sort do underline the need for great care in making an irrevocable decision and indicate that, just as with other contraceptive methods, tubal ligation too may have its drawbacks. Successful case histories can be quoted to argue the value of tubal ligation. Here is one example: Mrs. F. M., age 39, had a tubal ligation at the time of the delivery of her fifth child. The last two pregnancies had been unplanned and represented slip-ups in the use of a diaphragm and the condom. She had developed a severe dread of pregnancy, and her physical relationship with her husband suffered. Following tubal ligation and the assurance that she could not again become pregnant her attitude toward sexual relations improved. "A great weight was lifted from my mind." In the following years, though she experienced menopausal irregularities and would skip menstrual periods for several months, the knowledge that she could not be pregnant spared her much of the panic she had previously suffered in such circumstances.

Clearly, age may be a significant factor in weighing the merits of a tubal ligation. A woman approaching forty who has had several children must realistically face the fact that she is entering a period of diminished reproductive capabilities and may in fact be entering a period of relative or absolute infertility. Tubal ligation may therefore not represent a loss of a biological capability. Rather, it may present an answer to the problem of the "menopausal baby," with all the special complications that this may mean. The guarantee that tubal ligation gives against the possibility of pregnancy without the need for taking pills or using paraphernalia may be far and away the best solution. An even more clearcut instance where tubal ligation is applicable is with marriages where the offspring are for genetic reasons fated to be severely impaired or run the risk of early death, as may be the case with the presence of certain degenerative diseases of the nervous system which can be inherited.

A mother who has given birth to one or more such doomed children may be overwhelmingly anxious to avoid further pregnancies. If the defect is inherited from the husband's side rather than her own, she may be faced with the unfortunate dilemma of having to choose between having no children or giving up her marriage. A third alternative sometimes presents itself, namely donor or so-called artificial insemination. But if avoidance of pregnancy is desired, then tubal ligation may safely seal the decision. Because of the many delicate considerations involved in the sterilization procedure, it is always best for both parties in the marriage to reach a meeting of the minds and for both to assent willingly to the procedure. Indeed, it is customary for doctors to secure consent from the husband as well as the wife before performing tubal ligation.

Finally, it should be understood that other surgical procedures on the female reproductive tract may result in sterilization. Sometimes, because of infection involving the tubes and ovaries on both sides, large chronically infected sacs may result. These tubo-ovarian abscesses leave the whole structure incapable of reproductive performance and constitute a threat to the patient's health. She may suffer from repeated flare-ups of chills, fever, and debility. Although seen less frequently in this age of antibiotics, such abscesses do occur, and surgery is sometimes necessary. As a result of removal of the infected tube and ovaries, involuntary sterility may result. Similarly, removal of the uterus itself, though functioning tubes and ovaries are allowed to remain, will also lead to sterility since there is no place for the fertilized egg to develop. Actually, the break in the reproductive pathway produced by loss of the uterus also means that the sperm furnished by intercourse will never meet the egg.

Removal of the uterus may or may not be accompanied by removal of the ovaries. Opinions vary in this respect, and different procedures are followed by different surgeons. In the younger woman, it is customary to leave the ovaries in so that she can continue to receive the benefit of the hormones they secrete. In a woman approaching the menopause, it is customary to remove the ovaries at the same time that the uterus is removed, on the grounds that cessation of ovarian function is imminent anyway. From the menopause on, ovaries represent more of a threat from the point of view of possible tumor formation, a risk that may outweigh any conceivable benefit. Furthermore, it is also argued, if the effect of ovarian hormones is desired, it can easily be secured by resorting to pills or injections, and for as long as may be wanted.

There is an operation analogous to tubal ligation in women which can be performed on men, with equally successful outcome as far as sterilization is concerned. This is the procedure known as vasectomy. It is actually a good deal simpler to perform since no invasion of the interior of the body is necessary. The vasa, which are the two channels conducting the sperm upwards and outwards from the testis and epididymis, are readily felt in the male through the scrotum as firm cords. Ascending from the region of the testis towards the root of the penis, they are easily accessible to the surgeon.

The operative procedure is simplicity itself and can be performed in a few minutes. A small amount of local anesthetic is injected into the scrotum and two small incisions made, one on each side. Each vas is "fished out" through one of the tiny incisions, tied in two places, then cut between the two ties. Sometimes a small section of the vas is removed to further insure against the possibility of the cut ends growing together. Basically, the surgical procedure differs in no essential from that which is done on the fallopian tube, and leads to the same end result: an interruption in continuity of the channel so that the movement and meeting of the sex cells is blocked.

The comparative ease with which a vasectomy can be performed, and the absence of significant consequences after this essentially minor surgical procedure, should, one might suppose, make it a more widely used method. There is no impairment of sexual drive in the male, no interference with erection or secretion of the male hormone by the testicle. Essentially, nothing is changed except that soon after the operation no sperm will be found in the ejaculate when it is examined under the microscope. Despite the ease and potential usefulness of vasectomy, what the doctor most often encounters is a psychological obstacle. Some men, in every respect good husbands and responsible heads of families, balk at the idea of a vasectomy. They shrink at what appears to be an attack on their genitals, sometimes coming up with the most inadequate of reasons: "No tampering with my sex organs, doc!" Psychiatrists have thoroughly explored the many meanings and associations injury to the reproductive tract of the male has, so doctors know that however irrational a man's objection to vasectomy may be, it may constitute an unyielding reality. It is for this reason that most of the voluntary vasectomies have been performed on men who fall into a relatively intelligent and sophisticated group, in whom rationality triumphs over fears based on ignorance.

It is true that it may be difficult or even impossible to reverse a vasectomy, and as was noted above with tubal ligation, altered circumstances may sometimes make the male too wish for reversal of the sterilization procedure. Hooking together the two cut ends of the vas has in fact been done, but admittedly with only a low percentage of successes. In short, it is necessary for a man to be completely willing permanently to give up his potential for becoming a father when he undergoes a vasectomy, in much the same way that a still fertile woman gives up her potential for further motherhood when she has a tubal ligation. A man who has fathered four, six, eight, or more children and has a responsible attitude towards his obligation to rear and educate them may reasonably conclude that he has more than fulfilled his role as a father. If so, he can bypass more children by the vasectomy route.

It is of interest that very extensive campaigns based on vasectomy have been used to help control the population problem of India. Teams went out to Indian villages and performed vasectomies on the spot. The Indian government even went so far as to offer a bounty to all males undergoing vasectomy. But in India, as elsewhere in the world, it has become increasingly clear that the more willing and reliable of the two marital partners interested in curbing family growth is the woman. It is she who goes through the pregnancy, the labor, she who is most clearly responsible for the early nurturing and development of the offspring. The woman's stake in family planning is the greater. For this reason, the number of tubal ligations greatly exceeds the number of vasectomies—illustrating that the best hope for realistic answers to the world's population problems will be those provided by women.

It only remains to be said that new solutions to a problem are not always better than the older ones. There is much to be said for any well-established procedure whose pros and cons have been firmly determined with the passage of years. From this point of view, tubal ligation may be said to have many clear points of superiority over such rather new and untried contraceptive methods as the pill and the intrauterine device. For the woman or man capable of clearly considering all the facts, and one whose desire for parenthood has unequivocally been satisfied, sterilization by tubal ligation or vasectomy has much to commend it.

*The Control
of Fertility:
A WORLD
PROBLEM*

13.
Fertility on the World Scene

THIS IS A CENTURY of unprecedented turbulence, strife, and world wars, culminating in the invention of that most awesome and lethal of man's weapons, the atomic bomb. Revolutionary changes in the social order, combined with the catastrophic implications of the bomb, make all earlier problems in the international arena seem small to the vanishing point. And now another threat of equally grave proportions has crept up on us, unnoticed in the beginning because it was far more stealthy than any nuclear weapon. But it has now reached a threatening level. It's the problem of human fertility unchecked by what used to be considered natural means, the phenomenon popularly referred to as the population explosion. If we do escape nuclear warfare—whether by immobilization due to mutual terror or by some unlikely exercise of sanity—the world will be coming face to face with the massive consequences of a population it cannot possibly support.

Sex, Fertility, and Birth Control

The population explosion has none of the bursting violence of modern warfare. It is much easier to visualize the impact of A-bombs and H-bombs falling on great cities than to imagine the destructive effects that added millions of inhabitants have on these same cities. Particularly is this difficult for the people of a prosperous and economically expanding country like the United States. True, some of our slum areas seem to be more cluttered than ever with teeming humanity. But for those unwilling to put up with population changes in major cities and towns, an escape to the suburbs has long been an alternative. Yet with the passage of years even the suburbs begin to present a picture of increasing congestion. Empty spaces are disappearing, and one becomes increasingly conscious of being hemmed in by his neighbors. Enormous numbers of small children crop up and grow like Iowa corn in a good summer. Wrangles between "old settlers" and "new arrivals" over the building of schools and the floating of bond issues spring up. Finally, what had once seemed an adequate amount of land and open space is transformed into disorderly crowding, and people with motor cars come into conflict over parking spaces.

At the present rate of expansion, in the northeast United States alone we can look forward with assurance to a continuous population of human beings extending from Boston through New Haven and New York and on down to Baltimore and Washington. Essentially there will be continuity from one suburb to another, whatever the place differences implied by their differing names. This megalopolis will aggravate already existing problems, for all land will be covered with housing. It will assuredly worsen commuter congestion into the cities, the pollution problems of air and water, and even reduce the supply of streams and arable land, all despite the increasing outcry for conservation of land and space so that an occasional vista free of other peoples' houses can be preserved. However, we are lucky. All these problems in the United States are as nothing compared to the life and death problems accentuated by population expansion almost everywhere else in the world.

True, in the United States some of the problems raised by population expansion have had poor or inadequate answers. One of the most widely discussed, perhaps, has been that of the educational difficulties resulting from the rapid increase in the number of small children and teenagers. The problem has been compounded by the obsolescence of old schools requiring replacement, quite apart from the need for the building of new facilities. Crowded classrooms, double school shifts, hopelessly inadequate teacher-to-pupil ratios, and an obvious deterioration in standards are some of the notable consequences. The so-called baby boom that followed World War II is already making the problem acute at the high school and college levels, and the situation continues to worsen. Starting with 1964, each year *one million more high school graduates* are being turned out than five or ten years earlier. The Census Bureau indicates that there will be fifteen million students in high schools in 1970 as compared to ten million in 1960. Because of what has been termed the "revolution of rising expectations" as well as this increase in the school population, the problem at the college level will become even more marked. The Bureau of the Census forecasts a doubling of the number of college students from 1960 to 1970, and a further 50 per cent increase from 1970 to 1980. Thus the college enrollment picture, according to Donald J. Bogue, looks as follows:

YEAR	MILLIONS OF STUDENTS
1960	4
1965	6
1970	8
1975	10
1980	12

Of course, when we talk about the educational problems of high schools and colleges we have in mind a segment of the population which has higher incomes and standards of living than the submerged one-third or one-fourth. There are many millions of people crowded into the slums of our cities. With virtually all of them, higher levels of education and achievement simply are not part of their reckoning. The same can be said for the many millions who live in rural areas. They may escape the congestion of our cities, but they lead lives of equally blighted expectations and low achievement. From time to time some of these submerged millions may resort to violent protest, but for the most part their lives are spent in quiet desperation.

However, even the submerged third of our nation is housed and fed according to standards that would be regarded with genuine admiration by the countless millions in underdeveloped parts of the world. In the vast land and population areas that make up Southern Asia, the subcontinent of India, and Africa, hunger is an everyday reality or a never-distant threat. Malnutrition is chronic and widespread, and famine can number its victims by the tens of thousands. In Calcutta, India, more than 20 per cent of all families are confined to single rooms. Most have no running water and no toilet facilities, a situation typical of much of India, nonurban as well as urban. In Africa the situation is even worse. Here an important factor is a chronic deficiency of protein calories. This results in a disease of young children known as kwashiorkor, marked by stunted growth, retarded intellectual development, swelling of the extremities, and so poor a resistance to infections that a much higher death rate prevails among them. The widespread poverty of the underdeveloped countries leads to a fatalism and an acceptance of malnutrition, disease, and death that is quite incomprehensible to the visitor from the Western world. From the Western observer's point of view, life becomes dehumanized and the worth of all human beings is cheapened. What should be the abundant life becomes a painfully constricted existence. Human existence seems to take on a teeming, meaningless quality.

Faced with all this misery, one is truly overwhelmed by a feeling of the almost boundless capacity of human reproduction. No matter how high the death rate, it seems always to be exceeded by a still higher reproductive rate. If a couple have eight children and four die, they have nonetheless succeeded in doubling their own number. The net result is that a population which doubles in one generation will quadruple in two, and will increase sixteen-fold in less than a century.

What is ironic about the variations in human reproduction around the face of the globe is that precisely those who should be limiting their children are the ones least likely to have access to methods of contraception. The problems of introducing contraceptive methods to the illiterate rural masses of the great subcontinent of India are in themselves staggering. Equally great difficulties loom before the population planners in Latin America and the Caribbean region—in Puerto Rico, Jamaica, or Haiti. A Jamaican woman who has nine children in eleven years may not feel enthusiastic about having a twelfth or a thirteenth, but who will supply her with pills each month or teach her how to insert a diaphragm? Still, a massive and concerted effort to that effect must be initiated, or the already grave problem will become even more severe.

The Minister of Health of one underdeveloped country recently said to me, "Thanks to your help in the development of industry we are increasing our gross national product at the rate of 3 per cent per year. But our population is increasing at the rate of 4 per cent per year. Each one of us therefore is doomed to have less and less as the years go by." As Bertrand Russell has pointed out, because of the population growth of the last twenty years *human beings on the average are less well nourished* than they were before the Second World War. He goes on to say: "Of all the long-run problems that face the world, this problem of population is the most important and fundamental, for until it is solved, other measures of amelioration are futile." Eugene R. Black, speaking from the point of view of an economist, says: "Population growth threatens to nullify all our efforts to raise the living standards in many of the poorer countries. We are coming to a situation in which the optimist will be the man who thinks that present living standards can be maintained. A pessimist will not look even for that."

The plain fact is that we are in the midst of a crisis, a crisis due to human fertility. It is urgent. It is dangerous. It is also omnipresent. Put a pin through virtually any spot on the map outside of the Western world, and you will find a population crisis either already present or looming ominously. If your pin comes down in East Pakistan, for instance, you will find a situation well described by Irene V. Taeuber: "The population of East Pakistan was estimated at 53 million in 1961. In 1976, given the same conditions, it will be 84 million. More than 30 million people will be added in 15 years in a region without cities, industrial development, or substantial known resources or industrialization." For Egypt, this is what President Nasser has to say: "The population increase constitutes one of the most dangerous obstacles facing the Egyptian people in their drive for raising standards and production in their country in an effective and efficient way." The population of Brazil, estimated at 66 million in 1960, will be 98 million in 1975: 32 million more mouths to feed, bodies to clothe, minds to educate, in a generally impoverished country.

How did the world population crisis creep up on us so seemingly stealthily and rapidly? After all, it has been more than 130 years since Malthus wrote his celebrated essay predicting a crisis in which the population would outrun its food supply. The essay created a considerable impact in many circles. But no crisis of the kind he foresaw erupted in succeeding decades, and thus many of his statements and projections were discounted or negated. As it happened, many factors were operating to postpone the day of crisis he foresaw. Expanding population pressures in Europe and elsewhere could be siphoned off by emigration to a virtually still unpopulated New World. Then, as the eastern part of the United States developed and became increasingly populous, restless souls sought new frontiers to the west, eventually reaching the Pacific Coast. The ocean, of course, set the westward limit to the fanning out of the population here.

Famines and pestilence also played an important role in keeping human numbers down. The Irish potato famine of the 1840's killed millions. The great influenza pandemic of 1918-19 was estimated to have killed 18 to 20 million people as it spread around the world. Two world wars, each killing off millions of healthy young men in the full bloom of their manhood, were still another factor in lowering the potential levels of the population. But despite all these factors, there are others working in an opposing direction. Chief among these are the enormous and unprecedented medical advances which have reduced infant mortality to levels never before seen on the face of this planet. Where fifty years ago perhaps 10 to 20 per cent of all newborn children failed to attain their twenty-first birthday, improved sanitation, the advent of immunizations on a broad scale, and the introduction of germ-killing agents, such as the sulfa drugs and penicillin, have lowered the death toll literally by the millions. Children spared from diphtheria, scarlet fever, whooping cough, and bronchopneumonia were able to grow up, marry, and reproduce.

In addition to favorable influences affecting infant mortality, the same medical advances were similarly prolonging the life span of millions more: the teenager who might have died of meningitis, the young adult woman who might have died in childbirth, the middle-aged male who otherwise would have died of pneumonia, and so on. Death rates declined in all these age groups; life became less precarious; a family unit could count on continuing year after year instead of resigning itself to the prospect of unforeseen and unavoidable losses.

All these advances have had an even greater impact in the underdeveloped areas. In many of these, simply introducing DDT and elementary water purification meant adding millions of human beings to the sum total of the living. Unfortunately, this meant merely improving the quantity of life, not necessarily the quality of living. When combined with such changes as the shift from rural to urban life, new and unhappy patterns of life began to emerge. In many Latin American countries the pattern was represented by the appearance of shanty towns around the edges of larger cities, by mass unemployment, increased prostitution, and even a soaring death rate from abortions, as desperately unhappy women attempted to escape the burdens of still further pregnancies.

The prophecies of Malthus have become the brutal realities of today. At this very moment there are malnourished human beings lying down and dying in the streets of Hong Kong and Calcutta. What is inconvenient congestion in the Western world is a gnawing hunger in the underdeveloped world. A recent survey shows that North America, with 8 per cent of the world's population, has 23 per cent of the total agricultural production. In contrast the Far East, with 39 per cent of the world population, produces only 16 per cent of agricultural products. Nature has ruled that there must be cutbacks when a population exceeds its food supply, and there can be no exceptions. Mankind is on the point of seeing this brutal rule applied on a scale that may make the Irish potato famine seem very small indeed.

We have all been dimly aware of the growth of our own country's population, and secondarily of world population, during our own lifetime. But a longer-range view shows the process as more dramatic. It has been going on for centuries. In the days when Jesus trod the earth, the total world population is estimated to have been 250 million. Sixteen hundred years later, at about the time the Pilgrims landed on Plymouth Rock, this number had doubled to number 500 million. Then a sharp acceleration of the growth curve began. Two hundred years later, at the time Malthus worried about it, the world population was one billion. Today it is over three billion. In less than forty years another three billion will be added. So while it took hundreds of thousands of years for mankind to achieve the present total, the doubling of this number will now take place within only a few decades. No realist believes that intense exploitation of our present resources or a frenzied development of new ones can feed, clothe, and house another three billion human beings. This impossible rate of growth in one way or another will have to be stopped. As Irene V. Taeuber puts it, "Will growth be reduced through the humane processes of declining birth rates or the ruthless processes of increasing death rates?"

That human fertility should result in death, not life, is an inhuman paradox. The inevitable tragedy is simply made worse because of the Western tradition, born of Judeo-Christian ethics, which places such high value on human life and human fulfillment. If man is the lord of creation, made in God's image, and if human life is sacred, then the tragedy of the population explosion lies in its essentially anti-human character. When human beings swarm like flies, life becomes cheap. If it turns into a raw contest for calories of just any kind, for space of any dimensions, then the old great goals of individual development and maximum achievement are surely doomed. A full circle is about to be completed, with life again an elementary struggle for survival.

Not all individuals are willing to accept the results of

human sexual activity without a countereffort. One of the less happy solutions is, of course, abortion. In the United States this is an unpleasant, surreptitious, and occasionally dangerous solution—unless one is so fortunate as to have two psychiatrists affirm that one's mental health may be jeopardized by parenthood. However, in many countries abortion is legal and can be had for the asking. In Japan, a country which has successfully grappled with its fertility problems in recent decades, one informed estimate is that there are close to *two million abortions* per year (about twice the estimated number for the United States). Yet in an age where much is known about effective contraceptive techniques, an abortion rate of such dimensions is a tragedy and an unnecessary risk to women. There are better—and less drastic—solutions to the problem.

Pregnancy should be a cause for rejoicing, not a threat to living standards or to life itself. Many countries have clearly seen the choice they must make and have initiated efforts to escape the dangers of rampant human fertility. The World Health Organization, often working in conjunction with the UN's Technical Assistance Program, is doing a herculean job of spreading birth control information and setting up birth control clinics in the underdeveloped countries, where women from all walks of life can be instructed and fitted with intrauterine contraceptive devices (IUCD's). On the island of Taiwan alone, ten thousand such devices are distributed and inserted each month. Similar programs are being started in Hong Kong, India, Indonesia, and elsewhere.

Widespread acceptance and use of the IUCD or some similar contraceptive may help avert world disaster. Unfortunately, even where these devices are available, not enough women know about them or realize how simple, inexpensive, and effective they are. For, once properly inserted and retained (a small percentage of women are unable to retain them and must resort to other contraceptive methods) they are completely effective year after year, and need not be removed unless a pregnancy is desired and planned.

Clearly, a sharp reduction in pregnancy rate is the only solution to the problem of the population explosion. While some experts are a little more optimistic* than others —they feel that a larger world population can be supported at a reasonable level with the development of new resources such as atomic energy—all agree that the rate at which these resources can be developed must still inevitably lag behind the growth rate of the world's people, and that some sort of "breathing spell" is necessary so that the two rates of growth can be matched up.

The solution to the problems discussed here is not nearly so complicated as some have made it seem. The population explosion can be brought to an abrupt end if every married couple has no more than two children, and if the basic family unit is defined in terms of a grouping of four only. Once the possibility and the need for keeping the family unit at some such low level is incorporated into our social structure, we will have found the means for escaping the explosive possibilities inherent in present fertility trends.

14.
The Future
of Contraception

$\mathbf{I}$T IS TRULY SURPRISING how many of
the most important aspects of human health can be, and
indeed are, neglected over long periods. They then emerge
from obscurity and become the focus of sustained effort.
These odd shifts from virtually complete neglect to acquir-
ing the status of health problems of the first magnitude have
occurred so often that they must be the result of some special characteristic of human thinking. To give just one
example, mental disorders have been widespread and serious
for centuries. But they were neglected by both medicine
and the public, with the gravest consequences to the patients
suffering from them. Recently they have emerged from the
shadows to receive the attention and adequate study this
whole vast area deserves. After all, Sigmund Freud did not
invent the unconscious or its disorders; great pioneer though
he was, he merely described something that already existed
and was widespread.

Everything that may be said concerning mental illness and psychiatry is equally true of abortion and contraception. In the not too distant future the world will look back on our era in amazement at the shabby way we treated our womenfolk. Not only did we deny a woman the right to decide whether or not she should become pregnant, they will remark, but even in cases where pregnancy created a real threat to her health, only a criminal abortion surreptitiously performed was a possible solution—this including the teenage rape victim.

Although it can surely be maintained that family planning is an individual right and, like education, should be made accessible to everyone, information about it has been highly restricted and often legally forbidden. True, the richer or more intelligent or fortunate somehow always did have command of these resources when they wanted them, a situation which used to be cynically summarized in the phrase, "the rich get richer and the poor get children." This inequity is finally being rectified, though hardly at the most desirable pace. It is still too true that what should all along have been acknowledged as an individual's basic right is at last being granted to people on a broad scale by frightened governments trying to avoid the consequences of the population explosion. With ruin and desolation imminent— some might even say already here—first a slight stirring, then a more convulsive movement has occurred. Contraception is no longer a dirty word somehow associated with "lust." It now appears in print in our daily newspapers and can be openly mentioned on the radio and TV. At this rate of progress, it may shortly become a desirable practice for the sensible citizen in a sane society.

Foremost among the contributions to this rapidly changing scene has been the birth control pill. The pill has made contraception easy, acceptable, esthetic, and unprecedentedly reliable. It was the first real breakthrough in a field which had otherwise remained stagnant since the invention of the diaphragm around 1880. It did away with mechanical contraptions, tedious instructions, manipulations in squatting positions, or hurried maneuvers while in the grip of passion. Small wonder that despite its expense, some of its side effects, and even some of the remote threats posed by it, as by any newly introduced potent drug, the pill rapidly won the acceptance of millions in many lands. Its success has sparked new and energetic efforts to improve on the present version. The success of the pill makes it at least one of the signposts pointing into the future.

What will that future be? Since a future is inevitably the gestation product of the present, some predictions can be made about it even though the possibility of the unexpected has to be reckoned with, exactly as in any pregnancy. One thing that can be confidently anticipated is increasing social and governmental acceptance of the very concept of birth control. The process will be accelerated in part because of the newest advances. Already at the time of the Ecumenical Council in Rome in 1965 there were numerous predictions that endorsement of the birth control pill might be forthcoming. The celebrated Roman Catholic author of *The Time Has Come,* Dr. John Rock, speaking also as one of the co-discoverers of the pill, felt confident that it would be regarded as licit. Clearly the pill cannot fall under the previous bans forbidding the use of mechanical devices; but final questions as to its use by the orthodox still remain to be resolved, and at the highest level.

The mere fact that some of these questions can be discussed at length and the controversy aired publicly is in itself a sign of considerable progress. Even without the ban being lifted, the onward rush of events has swept aside some previous barriers. For the first time planned parenthood clinics are appearing in France; and in Latin America, where the matter is more urgent by far, birth control clinics are being publicly recognized and even supported by funds emanating from religious sources. Thus birth control programs have been set up within the last few years in Chile, Ecuador, and Venezuela, all only a few years following the appearance of the first such program in 1958 in Mexico City. Dr. J. Zañartu of Santiago, Chile, has been quoted as saying (*Medical Tribune*, May 21, 1966): "The largest birth control program in Latin America is being currently conducted in Santiago. Furthermore, this has the approval of the Catholic Church!" One measure of the grim state of affairs in Santiago has been the statistical finding, known also to be true in many other parts of the world, that the illegal abortion rate equals the natural birth rate—and the birth rate is one of the highest anywhere.

Although the rich and the influential may still debate the pros and cons of family planning, the necessity for it does not brook much delay. Here is a typical case cited by Dr. Edris Rice-Wray, founder of the first birth control clinic in Mexico City:

"Case I: Mrs. L.D.R. She is thirty-five, has nine living children, one an epileptic. Her husband, a part-time truck driver, earns an average of 650 pesos [about $52.00] monthly. She and her family live with her sister who has four children. Sixteen persons live in one room! She told us she had induced an abortion by taking herbs because she could not afford to have more children."

There is little need for multiplying typical illustrative case histories of this sort. Even so extreme a case as the thirty-year-old Mexican woman who had had thirty-one pregnancies, twenty-five of which were ended by abortion, simply points up the fact that there seems to be no limit to human fertility, human folly, and human despair. As is noted in Chapter 13, the massive increase in human beings is a world-wide problem, particularly accentuated in the underdeveloped countries, the very ones most in need of help. In many of these lands such difficulties with contraception as costs, problems in educating the masses, or religious hesitations will of necessity be swept aside.

It is altogether likely that new scientific achievements may simplify the problem still further. There are already a number of important investigations under way to indicate some of the probable lines for future development. Some of these are:

1. *The one-a-week pill:* Preliminary studies on a group of women in Mexico, sponsored by the Syntex Company, are indicative of one important line of endeavor. With this version of the pill, a single tablet is taken once a week. For a majority of women this appears to be sufficient to change the cervical mucus so as to produce an effective barrier against the sperm. As we have noted elsewhere (Chapter 3), the cervical secretion at the time of ovulation is thin, watery, and abundant, and favorable to penetration by sperm. Later in the cycle, however, it becomes more tenacious and thicker, and sperm penetrability is considerably diminished. In fact, even with the standard daily birth control pill there is evidence that the cervical secretions are altered in a manner unfavorable to sperm penetration; this change may be one of the several mechanisms of action of some of the current pills. With the new Syntex pill— and doubtless there will be others—it may be possible to produce a barrier to sperm entry without preventing ovulation or the other cyclic changes normally occurring in the ovary.

2. *The once-in-three-months injection.* It has been possible for many years now to produce injectable sex hormone compounds which are only slowly absorbed. After a single injection the compound may go on producing its effect for weeks, a prolongation of action known as the depot effect. Both male and female sex hormones of various kinds can be thus processed, with such convenient results as fewer injections, fewer visits to a doctor, and a steady prolonged level of hormone. In one recent study of a long-acting prod-

uct made by the Upjohn Company, a form of progesterone (the second hormone of the normal cycle) has been found to act exactly as the daily birth control pills do. The normal cycle in the ovary is inhibited, no egg develops, and the net effect is a once-in-ninety-days injection which acts as a contraceptive. Various other companies using similar long-acting preparations have also found that widely spaced injections can be useful birth control methods. Whether this approach will turn out to be as reliable as the standard pill remains to be determined.

3. *The morning-after pill.* As has been noted earlier (Chapter 2), the egg is fertilized in the fallopian tube. Following fertilization by the sperm, the egg slowly moves down the tube, taking approximately three days to traverse it. During this time changes in the ovary are occurring, and this prepares the uterus for the reception of a possible fertilized egg. There are a number of drugs which can be taken even after the egg has been fertilized to prevent the normal sequence of events. Thus it has been experimentally established in some animals that doses of the estrogens (the first hormone produced by the ovary during the normal cycle) can interfere with the usual journey of the fertilized egg down the tube and on into the uterus. The egg may not be able to pass on from the tube, a phenomenon known as tubal blockade; or if it does pass, it emerges into a uterus so altered as not to be suitable for implantation and further development. Some recent successful experiments have been performed with agents which prevent the development of the fertilized egg if they are taken for up to a week after intercourse. Interestingly these drugs, if taken past a critical time—for example once the egg has implanted—will not interfere with normal development. One way in which such a pill could be used would be for a woman to take it only for a few days after she has had sexual relations which might result in pregnancy. At other times there would be no need for taking any kind of pill.

Sex, Fertility, and Birth Control

Other pills, not based on hormone effects, have also been studied from the point of view of preventing normal development of the fertilized egg. Conceivably, some of the new pills used to destroy abnormal growths in the body may have an application against the developing embryo. At this point a delicate ethical and legal issue has been raised. It is this: that the taking of such a pill when a fertilized egg may already be in the tube (and there is no practical method of determining whether the egg has been fertilized or not at so early a stage) can be regarded as producing an abortion. There is one group of scientists and moralists who hold that the egg becomes a new human being as soon as it has been fertilized. Others hold that it is not a new human being until it has implanted in the uterus some nine or ten days later. The "morning after" pills produce their effect somewhere between fertilization and implantation. In certain special circumstances, such as after rape, a "morning after" pill might be a blessing. As compared with the other techniques, the "morning after" pill works only over a limited period, so that timing is a critical matter here.

4. *Antifertility pills for men.* The formation of sperm in the male is subject to hormonal control. It can be altered by hormones and other agents. Indeed, administration of the standard birth control pills to men will produce a decrease in their sperm count to the point of sterility. Unfortunately, in the male, such side effects as breast enlargement and tenderness rule out such pills as a practical method. Other hormonal agents, including male hormone itself, may at high-dose level also diminish sperm counts. From the practical point of view, none is as reliable at present as is the prevention of egg formation in women by means of existing pills. In the search for agents producing male infertility, various compounds have been examined, and several have been uncovered which result in complete abolition of sperm formation. Unfortunately, some of them

have side effects which may be potentially serious. Although there is every reason to expect that fairly safe pills for the male will eventually be found, it still remains problematic whether men will accept such agents. For a variety of reasons, a woman's motivation in this area is greater than a man's, and men psychologically seem to object to the idea of taking any agents which inhibit the formation of sperm. As Dr. Gregory Pincus, father of the birth control pill, has noted, sterilization procedures in females occur twenty times more frequently than similar procedures in males. This is true even though the operation in a woman may be a major one, whereas in the male it is a minor surgical procedure. Unless a really remarkable pill for the male is discovered, it seems likely that the control of conception will continue to be through agents taken by women.

Finally, the emerging new method of intrauterine contraceptive devices still remains one of the most promising areas for further development. The various problems and difficulties posed by these devices were discussed in Chapter 8. Despite the relatively recent introduction of the IUCD's, an accelerated process of evaluating them has occurred in recent years. New devices or modifications of existing ones are sure to yield safer and more effective successors. The fate of the IUCD's rests in some measure on the fate of birth control pills. If, for example, a simplified version of the pill, such as a once-a-week kind, does appear, there may be less need or demand for the IUCD. In any event, for women who cannot or will not take the pill, the IUCD may emerge as the most important of the practical alternatives.

Just as the IUCD modifies the uterine environment, in some manner making it unfavorable to the egg, so there is discussion of the possibility of altering the vaginal environment in a manner that will render it equally hostile to sperm. The observations of Dr. Masters and Mrs. Johnson have served to underline this possibility. They have found that in some women the vaginal secretions almost immediately kill off sperm. This "lethal factor" which produces sterility is unidentified, but its deadly efficiency is well attested to after careful observations. Unlike man-made vaginal contraceptive agents, the lethal factor does not need special measures to insure dispersal, seems to be present at all times, and has unrivaled efficacy in killing sperm.

The newly vitalized interest in this whole area gives promise of the development of new products which will be of greater efficiency and potentially wider use. Assuming that some major simplification is in the offing, as for example a once-a-week pill with little or no side effects or a permanently inlying intrauterine device which produces no other difficulties, the technical side of the contraceptive problem will have been largely solved. Experience with older and clumsier devices, such as the vaginal diaphragm, which have been largely restricted to the upper classes and to other favored groups, shows that birth control can and does work when the user is motivated. With the newer and better agents available, the problem is now becoming one of mass distribution and the simplification of measures so as to increase consumer acceptance.

More active government intervention in this area can now be expected. The governments of countries whose masses are poor or illiterate can establish acceptable approaches and measures, as experience in some Asian and Latin American countries has clearly shown. There are also unexploited mechanisms for exerting social and even financial pressure in this direction.

For instance, it is quite easy to foresee measures designed to make large families unfashionable and unpopular. Recent history in the United States attests to the importance of social and psychological factors in family size. Families with only one or two children were common during the Depression. Following World War II, three and four children became a popular number to have. In recent years a downtrend has again emerged. In the not too recent past, governments such as Mussolini's in Italy used to offer special bounties to families having extra children. A somewhat different version still persists in the United States— the income tax procedure which allows a $600 deduction for each dependent. It is easy to conceive of a shift in popular and governmental thinking which would abolish such allowances beyond a certain number of children. Of one thing we may be quite certain: family planning and population control are becoming imperative, and will eventually—probably sooner rather than later—become worldwide and universally accepted. Unrestricted and uninhibited human reproduction will become less and less socially permissible.

Index

Numerals in *italics* indicate illustrations and charts concerning the subject of the entry.

Index

Cervical and cervix (*cont.*)
  mucus, 74, 94, 122, 210
  polyp, 93
  secretion, *64*, 85
  wall, 57
Change of life. *See* Menopause
Child spacing, 17
  See also Family planning
Clitoris, 37, *53*, 54, *55*, 56, 57
Clocks. *See* Fertility calendars, clocks
Clotting. *See* Vein clotting
Coitus interruptus, 155
  psychological disadvantage of, 156
College enrollment, 197
Combined methods. *See* Birth control methods, combined
Condoms, 25, 27, 97, 108, 110, 114, 142, 160, 161, 177, 180
  defective, 28, 150
  psychological objections to, 101
Constipation, 125
Contraception and contraceptives, best, 118
  creams. *See* Creams
  future of, 206, 210
  jellies. *See* Jellies
  for newlyweds, 25, 161
  tablets. *See* Tablets
  See also Barriers; Birth control; Foams; Intrauterine contraceptive devices; Pill; Rhythm method
Cornified cells, 58, 75
Corpus (uterus), 57, 59
Corpus luteum, *64*, 66, *68*, 69, 75, *121*
C-quens (pill), 117, 122
Creams, 28, 102, 106, 109, 112, 114, 118, 151, 152, 153, 161
  efficiency ratings of, 115, 116
Cycles, anovulatory, 61, 67, 70
  charting of, 77, 81
  fertile phase of, 16, 168-169
    See also Fertility, maximum
  infertile phase of, 169
    See also under Safe period
  inhibition of, 119
  irregular, 170, 178

  long, 177, 178
  "normal," 26, 123
  regular, 30, 79, 170, 172, 173
  short, 71, 178
  See also Menstrual cycles

Death rates, 199, 202, 203
Defloration, 54
Delfen Cream, 115, 152
Depot effect, 210
Depression (economic), 23
Depression (psychological), 122, 125
Diabetes, 31, 133
Diaphragm, 27, 28, *103*, 108, 109, 112, 113, 114, 135, 137, 142, 143, 161, 177, 186, 188, 199, 208, 214
  after childbirth, 149, 151
  dislodgement of, 110, 149, 150, 151, 153
  fertility after using, 24
  fitting of, 102, 104, 105, 151, 158, 160
  impossibility of loss of, 24, 25
  need for change of, 104, 105
Digestive disturbances, 125, 133
Dizziness, 125, 126
Donor insemination. *See* Artificial insemination
Douching, 58, 99, 111, 112, 113
  disadvantages of, 157

Ectopic pregnancy. *See* Pregnancy, ectopic
Eggs, *68*, 79, 157
  fertilization of, 183
    See also Fertilization
  maturation of, *64*, 65, 70, 71
  pathway of, *62*, *184*
  wastage of, 71
Ejaculation and ejaculatory ducts, *43*, 44, *46*, *51*, 52
Embolisms, 127, 128
Emko Vaginal Foam, 115, 152
Enovid (pill), 117, 122, 128
Epididymis, *41*, *43*, 44, 190
Epilepsy, 31
Erections, 40, 48, 49, 50, 52, 144, 190
Erogenous zone, secondary, 37

Index

Index

Index

Thermal shift, 79, *80*
  effect of illness on, 81
  and timing of intercourse, 80
  and timing of ovulation, 77, 78
Thermometer. *See* Ovulation thermometer
Thrombosis, 128
Thyroid disorders, 93, 130, 131
Tietze, Christopher, 83
Time Has Come, The, 208
Triplets, 71, 93
Tubal and tubes, blockade, 71, 93, 211
  infection, 189
  ligation, 183, *184*, 188, 189, 191, 194
    advantages of, 185, 187
    disadvantages of, 186 187, 188
    patency test, 93
    pregnancy. *See* Pregnancy, tubal
    removal of, 189, 190
    restorative surgery for, 186,
Tumors, 30, 132, 133, 161
  See also Fibroids
Twins, 93
  the pill and, 24

Underdeveloped countries, 134, 135, 204, 209
United Nations Technical Assistance Program, 204
Unplanned pregnancy. *See* Pregnancy, unplanned
Unsuspected pregnancy. *See* Pregnancy, unsuspected
Urethra, female, *53*, 56
  male, *39*, *43*, 44, *46*, 47, 50, *51*
Urinary system, male, 50, *51*
Urine examination, female, 75-76, 89
Uterine and uterus, 55, 57, *62*, 63, 66, *103*, 127, *184*, 185
  cancer, 129
  cavity, *57*, *60*

  congestion, 74
  infection and inflammation, 138, 139
  lining, 24, *57*, 59, *60, 64,* 66, 67, 120, 140
  position of, 148, 149
  removal of, 189
  varicose veins, 148

Vagina and vaginal, 37, 50, 52, *53*, 54, *55*, 56, *57*, 59
  acidity, 58, 145
  canal, 57
  congestion and expansion, 145, 146, 148, 149
  discharge, 74, 79, 85
    See also Vaginal lubricating fluid
  foaming tablets. *See* Tablets
  foams. *See* Foams
  infections, 74, 94
  lining, 58, *64*, 74, 75
  lubricating fluid, 145, 149, 152
  suppositories. *See* Suppositories
  wall, *55*, *57*, 58, *103*, 146
Varicocele, 92
Vasa, 190
Vasectomy, 190, 192
  psychological obstacle to, 191
Vault (vaginal), 58
Vein clotting, 30, 31, 127, 128, 133, 161
Vestibule (vaginal), *53*, 54, *55*, 56
Virginity, proof of, 54
Vollman, Rudolf, 81
Vulva, *53*, 54, 56

Washington University School of Medicine, 144, 149
Weight gain, 122, 125, 130
Womb. *See* Uterus
World Health Organization, 204
Wright, Irving, 128

Zañartu, J., 209

224